AD

13 Years Lost is a poignant and heartfelt story of the strength and resilience of the human spirit that kept me reading well after bedtime. Thank you Christine, and peacekeepers of the world, for your service to humanity.

—**MONA CEURVELS,** *Life Enrichment Coordinator, The Arlington of Naples*

I devoured this immensely readable book in a single sitting. *13 Years Lost* will leave you feeling energized and charging off to the nearest airport to experience your own adventures.

—**KELLY SMITH,** *Deputy Representative UN Office Drugs & Crime, Afghanistan*

This is a book that you will not be able to put down, about a woman who would not accept defeat.

—**HELEN POWERS,** author, model

This powerful story of a woman seeking love, but also learning to depend on herself, moved me to tears. It's also a beautiful love story of Christine's journey and connection with her soulmate.

—**PATTI PRITCHETT,** *childhood friend*

This is a message of hope and faith in humanity. It is also a call to action for justice so that all may live, love and share – as individuals and collectively as humans.

—**MARCO KALBUSCH,** *German Lawyer, Physician*

Christine's memoir is an inspiring read for anyone striving to overcome adversity.

—**KATHLEEN PELLECCHIA,** *Claims Taker, Social Security Administration;*
Vice President, American Federation of Government Employees

Christine Sadry's autobiographical *13 Years Lost* is a testament to resiliency. Quite a read!

PAMELA GIRTMAN, *President, Circumnavigators Club, Naples Chapter,*

Christine did not let her past define her future. I will be buying this book as a gift for my friends to read.

BARB BECHTOLD, *friend and former co-worker at Social Security Administration*

Christine tells her story of hardship, friendship and triumph with love, insight and wisdom. You will find yourself eager to turn each page to experience the excitement, sense of accomplishment, and sheer fun of being part of a peacekeeping mission.

PIPPA BURGESS-ARCOS, *retired United Nations Staff*

Sadry writes about her amazing life journey and looks openly at important human themes: how we wound and are wounded by those we love; the identity conflict that many immigrants feel; and the horrendous suffering in many countries around the world. Most importantly, Sadry shares strategies for maintaining balance when surrounded by human suffering, while relating the beauty and benefits of traveling the road to forgiveness.

ALAN KELLER, *former Deputy Director, Africa Division of United Nations Population Fund (UNFPA); former Director of UNFPA Country Support Team for Southern Africa*

13 YEARS
LOST

Scan to watch Christine share
some of her amazing stories.

13 YEARS
LOST

An Unbelievable Story of Fleeing
Communist Poland to Traveling the
World Serving the United Nations

CHRISTINE SADRY

O'LEARY
PUBLISHING
The Influencer's Press

NAPLES, FL

ISBN: 978-1-952491-82-5 (print)
ISBN: 978-1-952491-83-2 (ebook)
Library of Congress Control Number: 2024919336

Editing by Orla Fagan and Heather Davis Desrocher
Line Editing by Kat Langenheim
Proofreading Boris Boland
Cover and interior design by Jessica Angerstein
Printed in the United States of America

This book is dedicated to two remarkable souls who have illuminated my path, enriched my life, and shaped the very essence of who I am.

First, my beloved grandmother – whose unwavering strength, determination and resilience served as a beacon of inspiration throughout my life. And my loving husband – whose steadfast support, calming presence and understanding have been my constant anchor.

Contents

Our Stories, Our Lessons

As I began documenting my life experiences, it dawned on me that I was writing the core of my being onto the pages of this book. The challenges I confronted seemed to escalate with each passing moment; it was as if I was an avid reader engrossed in a narrative that was undeniably my own. It started with the decision to write down my thoughts on paper. It was a revelation that not only unveiled this book, but also unfolded my life.

As I was writing, I had an epiphany that struck me like a lightning bolt: I was composing a narrative that extended beyond myself. In my tapestry of trials and tribulations, I recognized the universality of the human experience. The hurdles we surmount and the lessons we learn resonate within the

1

collective human spirit. With this realization, I understood the importance of sharing my story.

As a 9-year-old child from Poland, stepping onto a foreign shore alone, with nothing but courage in my heart, I was propelled by a hunger to explore, understand, and be captivated by the world's experiences. Little did I know that this journey would etch itself into the fabric of my soul. I never once took my position and privilege for granted while working in some of the toughest corners of the world; and there were many times I could identify with the hardships that people were experiencing.

I have also come to realize that I have lived not just one lifetime, but multiple lifetimes – every phase more complex, each challenge more demanding, and each experience a stepping stone toward self-discovery. Through it all, the fire within me never dimmed. I embraced the unknown, taking risks that some might have shied away from.

My life has been mixed with great sadness and great joys, with lessons learned from good, bad and heartbreaking moments. But within these experiences, a truth emerged – life is a continuous voyage; an ongoing exploration that knows no bounds. As long as we draw breath, we have the opportunity to encounter, to absorb, and to evolve.

These pages are a glimpse into my journey through life's unpredictable landscape. It is a testament to the fact that within each of us resides the power to overcome obstacles, triumph over challenges, and pursue passions and aspirations. From facing seemingly insurmountable hurdles to basking in the glow of achievements, I have lived a life of authenticity, driven by intuition and a belief in the adventure itself.

I have been tested to the very core of my being. There were times I questioned my choices and wondered about the roads I did not take. But on reflection, I realized that my journey was uniquely mine. I have been shaped by the decisions I made in pursuit of my dreams, guided by my heart's compass. I am grateful for the roads I have traveled and the lessons I have learned. I may not have achieved what society deemed enough. Still, I have dared to create my destiny, triumph over adversity, and welcome the unknown.

My intention is that these pages will serve as a reminder to take on life fully, chase your passions relentlessly, and believe in your ability to overcome obstacles. I hope these words inspire you to confront challenges with unwavering courage and to seize every opportunity, with a heart open to boundless beauty. There is a world of experiences waiting for you to discover. May my story inspire you.

To my dearest family and my beloved friends, my rendition of the past might not perfectly mirror your perspective. Nuances may differ in retelling our shared story, but the essence remains true.

I acknowledge my own shortcomings. Weaving my mistakes into a narrative became an essential facet, one that invited introspection and growth. It is my sincere hope that even in the tragic chapters, a compassionate lens will be used to view the choices I made, recognizing the intricacies that make us all human. This chronicle is a testament to the resilience that is inherent in all of the lessons that adversity bestows.

Poland

L ife, indeed, can push us to our limits – testing our strength and resilience. From my earliest days, born into a modest family in a communist country, I faced challenges that seemed insurmountable. But those were just the beginning. Life continued to throw hardships my way, each one more daunting than the last. Yet, it is not the hand we are dealt that defines us, but how we choose to play it. This is a story of one little girl who crafted an extraordinary life, against all odds. It is my story; but in its essence, it is the story of every human being who has ever fought to rise above their circumstances and find hope in the darkest of times.

I was born Krystyna Danilowicz in rural Communist Poland. I was reared on a small farm in the northeast corner of the country, in the village of Krasne, where I lived with my family. Nestled alongside the shores of Lake Dlugie in the northeast, the remote hamlet was shaped like a horseshoe. In the 1950s, this tightly knit community consisted of around 20 houses. Ours was in the middle of the horseshoe, where the front of the house overlooked our vegetable garden and the rear of the house backed up to a pine forest.

I was just 5 years old when my maternal grandmother, Helena, was left to take care of my baby sister, my older siblings, and me while my mom was admitted to hospital for an operation. It was a weekday, and Grandma had dispatched my older siblings off to school that morning. She had ensured that they had their homework completed and that there was a packed lunch in their school bag. My father was working, tending to the animals from the very early morning. He had left the house with a hot drink in a flask and food that he would eat when he got to the farm. He and my grandmother had little to say to each other; and with spring on the way and the lambing season about to begin, the few animals we possessed required his full attention. If an animal died during the birth process, it would be a great loss for our family's meager resources.

Grandma was staying home with us younger ones; she cleaned, cooked and baked for the family in my mother's absence. I was helping with the chores, doing my best to assist and ease Grandma's burden. Even at such a young age, I was aware that my grandmother's advancing years impeded her ability to accomplish household chores in the way my mother could before she became ill.

It was mid-morning when my eldest sister arrived home, shattering the peace of the house and taking Grandma by surprise. She was not due home until much later in the day. Grandmother was outside in the yard, washing cloth diapers and clothes in a big tin vessel that doubled as our bath on the weekends. My sister, who was 11 years old at that time, came through the gate sobbing so hard that she was almost hysterical. She was incoherent in her grief. Grandma rushed over and put her arms around the distressed child, trying to understand what was making her so upset.

Through her sobs, my sister eventually made herself understood. Grandma heard the words repeated over and over, "Mama is dead. Mama is dead. Mama is dead." The words sunk in as my grandmother realized that her dear youngest daughter had passed away in the hospital. Her jaw dropped and she began asking questions about who, how, why, and what had happened, before the news really registered. Then, a low howl of grief started in her abdomen, reached a fevered pitch – and ultimately spewed from her throat, echoing across the village and far into the fields. She ran out onto the street screaming, "Wanda is gone. Wanda is dead." Her keening and tears of anguish brought the other women out of their homes, gathering around her. Once the severity of the news became obvious, one of the neighbors ran to the fields, looking for my father to inform him of the shocking news.

I stood among the dozen or so neighbors who had gathered around us and were almost smothering me. I felt as though I were absorbing my grandma's and sister's raw grief as I gazed up at them, trying to comprehend what had happened and what they were saying. I could grasp words here and there, but it didn't yet add up in my young brain that my mother was never going to return home. I can remember thinking, "Why is grandma crying? Grandmas do not cry, children cry; and the grandmas' job is to console children, not to cry themselves."

I couldn't come to grips with what was going on around me. All the women were crying, so I began to cry too – I was upset because they were upset. We stood there for a long time before Grandma went back to the house to prepare herself. One of the neighbors came into our house as my grandmother went out, and she waited until my father made it home. In a remote community like ours, communication was difficult, and Grandma needed to contact my mother's siblings and her cousins to let them know the news.

As I look back on that momentous event, I realize it was the most defining moment of my life. To this day, I can still recall the devastation of the village women when we heard that my mother, a young woman in her 30s, was gone, never to return. It changed the trajectory of my life dramatically, and led me to a life that would be impossible to imagine – one that would take me across vast oceans, separated from all that I once knew and loved, and all those I held most dear. It was the beginning of the end, and it would lead to 13 years lost, where I encountered suffering at the hands of evil and brutal people, until I found my way home again.

World War II

As Western Europe gained its freedom at the end of World War II, eastern Europe, including Poland, fell under the oppressive control of the Union of Soviet Socialist Republics (USSR). On September 1, 1939, Hitler had begun a campaign to dominate Europe by invading Poland from the West; 16 days later, the Soviet Union invaded Poland from the East on a pretense to "protect" Ukrainians and Belarusians living in Poland's eastern regions. Caught between these two great powers, Poland endured six years of devastating conflict, culminating in the defeat of Nazi Germany in 1945.

Yet, instead of liberation, Poland would be shrouded in a long, dark shadow as Moscow's brutal rule denied Poles autonomy and democracy. The Iron Curtain was drawn. For those of us born in the postwar era, the future appeared bleak, filled with nothing but grinding poverty and hardship. It offered little hope, and even less comfort.

In such a grueling, horrific environment, Polish people sought comfort through their religion. As many as 99 per cent of the population identified as Catholic; they clung to the comfort of their faith, assured by the clergy that their suffering would be rewarded. There would be a joyous reunion with their Maker in the afterlife. Although the politburo in Moscow practiced an unofficial policy of state atheism with an aim to eliminate religious belief, it never made any moves to ban religious practice, and Poland remained deeply Catholic.

As a child in a postwar environment, I never heard the war discussed. However, from a very young age, I was aware that we were locked behind the Iron Curtain. With that in mind, I think people across the country had a great hesitancy to question anything, for fear of reprisals. I have a clear memory of wandering off into the fields near my home and seeing Soviet tanks conducting military exercises. Hundreds of armed soldiers had gathered. I stopped dead in my tracks, unable to move. I was mesmerized by these war games and wracked by the fear that we were coming under attack. After staying hidden for the longest time, I raced back home, sobbing, to tell my family what I witnessed.

Compared to city folk, my family did not experience much of the trauma brought about by the conflict. In a sense, we were lucky that we lived in the country, although we experienced our own hardship that comes with isolation and poverty. While Poland was trying to rebuild in the aftermath of six years of bombardments from both sides, the majority of Polish people were employed or worked on the land. To this day, Poland remains a rich agricultural land, where fields of golden wheat stretch beyond the horizon. In the 1950s, life was probably a lot tougher in the cities – parts of

Warsaw, Kraków, and other big urban areas had been razed to the ground. Comparatively, life in the countryside continued as before.

My mom, Wanda, was born in 1926, and my dad, Stefan, two years earlier. They had married just after the war, settled into farming my grand-mother's small holdings, and started a family. I came third in the family, and my early childhood days were filled with the domesticity of rural life. I lived in harmony with my siblings, my mom, and my grandmother, Helena Moroz. It was mainly a family of women, as my father was never much present, largely keeping himself busy outside the home. When he was home, I can vaguely recall that there was tension. I have no clear memory of him – good, bad, or indifferent – or of ever meeting his family, my paternal grand-parents, aunts, uncles or cousins. Whether my father fought in the war or not, it was never mentioned. He was an elusive figure in our lives.

We lived in a simple, two-room house – one room was used as a bed-room, and the other was the living and kitchen area. No one in the village had electricity or the luxury of running water; but we were lucky enough to have a well close to the house that provided all our water needs. The only time I remember that we couldn't use the well for drinking water was when a cat fell into the well. I can recall the commotion it caused at the time, and I'd love to be able to tell you the cat was rescued and survived; but alas, that part of the event has been erased from my childhood memory.

Winters in Poland were harsh, with little daylight and gray skies for months on end. Snow was heavy and drifts were severe. Sometimes, we were prevented from even opening the door of the house, as several feet of snow would be pressed up against it. Frequently during the winter months, we would awaken to see icicles formed on the inside of the windows, and our breath would be visible in the cold air. Siblings shared beds; sleeping next to each other had the added benefit of keeping us warmer. For even more warmth, we used our winter coats like extra blankets.

The kitchen stove was the only means of heating the house during those dark, gray, bitterly cold winter months. Keeping warm in the house required much jostling to be close enough to the stove. The dexterity and skill this required could have been declared a national sport. We longed for the end of each winter and greeted the arrival of the long days of summer with joy.

Summer temperatures were never too hot; we benefited from the cool breeze that came off the lake. It acted like a natural air conditioner, keeping temperatures at a comfortable level. Summer also provided some memorable, carefree childhood days, which included swimming in the lake and playing street games with other kids from the village.

My maternal grandfather was dead by the time I made my arrival in the family, so my father, as the only male, was relied upon to do the heavy farm work on our grandmother's land. Our lives centered around the farm, so we were aware of nature and recognized its forces. Living in the country, I believe that we had a heightened awareness of the seasons, the animals, and growth in nature. When spring popped its head around the corner, it brought with it hope for new life and rebirth. The children were expected to help in the market garden, and from a young age my sisters and I were involved with springtime planting and fall harvesting.

However, all productivity, especially the buying and selling of farm produce, was controlled by the local Communist Party. Each farmer was obliged to hold a party membership card and apply for permission to sell what they produced. Otherwise, they could be liable for some harsh penalties. Indeed, farming wasn't a particularly profitable venture, but the extra money earned from selling produce beyond our income requirements was used for household essentials. There was never a shortage of food, because we had several cows, pigs, sheep and chickens.

Farming in Poland was organic then, and I can still remember the taste of the full-cream milk we used in our tea, the distinct smell and flavor of the tomatoes in the days before they were genetically modified, and the richness of the eggs that we gathered from the chicken coop. With an abundance of wheat available, many women – my grandmother included – were skilled at making bread. The smell would waft through our small house as we would wait in eager anticipation of mealtime.

We were blessed to have fruit trees – apple, pear, cherry and plum. We also had a strawberry patch and bountiful blueberries. The vegetable garden was the women's domain, and they grew cucumbers, carrots, lettuce and cabbage. I have clear memories of the flowers we grew – especially the peonies, which would bloom in early spring. The peonies signaled the end of winter and promised long summer days ahead. The peonies were gathered from the garden and all sorts of containers were used as flower vases for them, which allowed the distinct, sweet aroma to waft through the whole house.

Sundays were special. My mother would make our favorite meal, *kielbasa and sauerkraut*, a highly flavored sausage of pork shoulder with salt, pepper, garlic and marjoram. Each household had their own version of *kielbasa,* with varying herbs and spices in recipes handed down from generation to generation.

Sunday mass was obligatory for every Catholic. Failure to attend was a sin on your soul that came with the threat of an afterlife burning in hell. And the church's promise of a better life in the next world ensured that no one crossed the line or rebelled. We knew nothing else besides Catholicism. Obeying God's law and the priest's interpretation of dogma determined whether a family would receive grace and favors to reach heaven. The priest dictated how each community should live their lives.

My grandmother and her children
Helena, Wanda and Henryk

The church where we prayed as a family is still standing in the neighboring village of Krasnopol. My maternal great-grandfather's headstone, dating back to 1865, still remains in the adjoining cemetery. During every occasion, from weddings to baptisms to funerals and Lenten prayers, the smell of incense filled the church. To this day, when I pass a room where incense is burning, I'm brought back to the village church in Krasnopol, where I felt God had graced us with his or her presence.

My mother Wanda was the youngest of three children; she had an older sister, Helena, and a brother, Henryk. They were a close family, but poverty drove my grandparents to leave the village before the war with their children to seek work in France. They stayed there more than a year, but struggled to find work. When the simple act of survival in a foreign land became too difficult, my grandfather decided that it was better to be poor at home. So, the family returned to the familiarity of Krasne, unaware of the life-changing events about to overtake Europe.

During their time in France, my aunt Helena became fluent in the language in a short space of time. That served her well when she became a French school teacher in Poland. Back home, Henryk, my uncle, excelled at school; and on finishing high school, he immediately left for Krakow and the university there. No one could ever blame Henryk for wanting to escape a village where there was no local school beyond fourth grade, no primary health care facilities, no doctors, and no stores to buy even the most basic of items. Henryk went on to become a mathematics professor and later became dean of the Jagiellonian University in Kraków. He was a source of pride, and a celebrity among the family and the village.

Grandmother not only baked great bread; she was also an accomplished seamstress and knitter. Each year, the sheep would be rounded up for shearing; their wool would then be treated and spun into yarn and wool. Clothes would be crafted directly from my grandmother's hands; for winter, she knitted sweaters, gloves, hats and blankets. Clothing was handed down from older sister to younger sister, so by the time the summer dresses and winter woolens reached me, they were well worn and often creatively patched.

Mom was a petite woman with sharp features and a backbone of iron; her commitment to her children and her home were unquestionable. Home and family formed the center of her universe. We were a family of girls, and I came in after Elzbieta (Ela) and Teresa, with Joanna making an appearance a few years later. Mom had seven pregnancies, but with the lack of available reproductive healthcare for women, just four girls survived beyond the first year.

I have no recollection of Joanna's arrival into our home, although I was 4 years old at the time. I do have, however, a very vivid memory of my sister Basia, who was born before Joanna. Basia became ill not long after she was born. Despite my grandmother's efforts – making potions from herbs to address Basia's health issues – she had no success. In the end, they decided that what my sister required was her vaccinations. So, accompanied by Grandma, my mother carried Basia to the bus – a trek of two mile s– to get the baby to the clinic. Believing that the vaccinations would be sufficient to cure the baby, they all returned home. But within a short time, Basia developed diarrhea. Her little body just could not cope, and eventually she succumbed in her fight for life.

Basia was dying from early in the morning until midday. In a letter from my mom to her brother Henryk in Krakow, she described how I became hysterical, begging her to close the doors and windows to stop the baby from going to heaven. I can still see myself kneeling at Basia's white coffin in the tiny, windowless room in the church. I tried to comprehend the concept of death as it related to my baby sister, who had lived just three short weeks. In the letter my mother sent to Henryk, she described how the doctor had misdiagnosed Basia's bronchitis. I know that in 1986, the infant mortality rate in Poland was 19.3/1000,[1] so I imagine the rates in the 1950s and '60s were abysmal.

Basia was not the first child that my mother had lost. Mom also buried two boys; one just eight weeks of age and the other three months old. As a caring and loving mother, it must have been heartbreaking for her; but the reality of a tough rural life left no time to grieve. She had farm chores, the house, and her girls to contend with – she had no choice but to carry on. I believe that my mother's strong religious faith helped her to cope with those awful tragedies – she always accepted her situation without complaint.

My memory of her is one of a loving mother who protected her children with the ferociousness of a lioness – everything was for her girls. Mom worked in the home with no modern appliances, but she could turn the most basic of foods into a tasty, hearty family meal. This was also in the days before disposable diapers, so my mother washed our diapers and other clothes by hand in a large tin bathtub, perched on a table outside the back door.

The kitchen stove was a beast. It required constant feeding with firewood and coal; and if it became extinguished, there was consternation. Trying to relight the only source of heating and cooking in our home was difficult.

My mother was up from dawn to dusk. When she was not working in the home and raising four daughters, she was planting, sowing and reaping on our farm. In a letter to Henryk, she spoke about harvesting potatoes, beets and *rutabagas* (similar to turnips), and about bringing the crops in to preserve for the winter months. In the fall, when the wild berries along the hedgerows ripened, she would go out with us children and the other village women and children to collect the berries, which were turned into delicious jams. Nothing was wasted in our home; everything was repaired and reused

---

1 https://pubmed.ncbi.nlm.nih.gov/12177960/

until it was physically impossible to fix or mend. What we lacked in material things, we were more than compensated with our mother's care, empathy, love and protection.

The remoteness of the village meant that we had no access to public transport or communications. There were no telephone lines into the village; so, even if someone could have afforded it, no house in the village could have been equipped with a phone. Getting to the nearest bus stop meant a hike of more than a mile along an unpaved country lane. During the winter months, the lane became impassable. Snowdrifts made leaving the village impossible, and isolation from the world became complete. School for those attending fifth grade and above involved a three-mile hike or taking a bus. The walk to and from school was tough going for children, and it took an hour to hike each way when there was decent weather.

I was 4 years old when I made my first trip outside our village, to visit a dentist. In my short, sheltered life up to that point, it was a momentous occasion for me. My mother and I took the bus to Suwalki. Not only did it provide a thrilling respite from humdrum farm life, it also sparked a curiosity within me to explore and experience life beyond the boundaries of Krasne.

It was the first time I had ever seen gypsies. A group had gathered in the park close to the bus stop in Suwalki. I found their colorful clothing and tambourines mesmerizing as they sang and danced with abandon. The excitement of the trip, however, soon dissipated when the visit to the dentist proved to be an unexpected ordeal. In communist Poland, anesthesia was a privilege afforded only to the rich; because we were poor, my tooth was simply yanked out. The extraction was done with such a painful force that it elicited an earth-shattering scream and enough tears to fill the nearby lake to overflowing.

Once the tooth was out, though, the doctor gave me a lollipop to assuage the shock and pain. I think it may have been the first time I had ever tasted a lollipop, and the luxury of such a treat proved successful in slowing my tears. The candy ultimately allowed me to continue enjoying my trip; an added benefit was having my mother all to myself for a whole day.

Grandmother, Mother, Ela, Krysia and Teresa

The close-knit feeling of community was at the heart of village life. Every family was in the same situation, all struggling for daily survival and trying to make ends meet. Despite the circumstances, each neighbor was there to help when trouble came knocking at the door. And indeed, there were no such things as locks and keys – the door to each home in the village remained open to neighbor or stranger.

The village was an extension of the family. While individual families had their own struggles, as a community we had come together with an indomitable human spirit that transcended all the hardship we faced each day. The old adage – "What doesn't kill you will make you stronger" – comes to mind. It was almost like an unspoken mantra for the life that lay ahead for me.

It was 1960, and I was 5 years old when my mother began experiencing pain. I first noticed it one day while my two older siblings were at school; only 8-month old Joanna and I were at home. Right in the middle of a task, Mom would suddenly double over, clutching her stomach, unable to move. I can still picture her lying on the bed, crying silently; her skin had gradually turned yellow and she was crouched in a fetal position, overwhelmed by the pain that wracked her body.

Similar incidents continued for a long time before she gathered us one morning to explain that she needed to go to the hospital and that she would be away for several days. She smiled, trying to lighten the mood, and I can remember her embrace as she kissed and hugged each one of us. She promised that she would return before we even missed her presence.

The shortage of medical resources in our small village was a harsh reality. The nearest doctor resided miles away. With little or no public transport, he could only be reached by using a horse-drawn cart that was primarily reserved for farm activity. The doctor immediately recommended that my mother undergo surgery and she was taken to the hospital in Bialystok, 78 miles from our village. But there was no communication available between our remote village and the outside world – no telephone, no telegram, nothing. We could not have been more isolated if we lived on Mars, let alone in the heart of Europe. My mother was 34 years old the day she left our home to go to Bialystok for a simple gallstone operation.

In my mother's absence, Grandma tried to minimize the disruption in our daily routine – getting Ela and Teresa ready for school, cooking meals, and keeping the house tidy. We kids were given chores to help out, but the bulk of the responsibility fell on my grandmother's shoulders. Each morning, there seemed to be a few more worry lines etched on her face.

As the days rolled into each other and no news arrived, the atmosphere at home grew increasingly tense. Despite Grandma's every effort to keep us upbeat, it was impossible to shake the growing sense of doom. Joanna was still very much a baby at the time and I was the preschooler, so both of us were home with grandma. Ela and Teresa, as usual, went off to school.

It was a normal morning for Ela; she was sitting among her peers in fifth grade. The school director – a stern, imposing man whose gray clothes matched his dour nature – barged through the door, interrupting the class. Standing at the top of the room and without preamble, he announced to the entire class of 11-year-olds that he had received a phone call that Ela's mama had passed away.

The announcement was blunt and tactless, devoid of any empathy or sympathy. Because the school was the only institution between Bialystok and Kranse with a telephone, the call announcing the unthinkable had been placed to the school. Ela sat in the class, stunned, trying to absorb the news. The director pointed to her, barking an instruction to "go home."

Our dear mother was dead, and our little family's world collapsed like a child's sandcastle hit by a tidal wave. It would be years before Ela spoke about the unwanted attention from her peers, who were both curious and intrigued at the announcement. To them, it was news that they could take home to be discussed and dissected around the dinner table with family. Ela's naked grief was on display for the school as she walked the long corridor towards the exit. Trying to make herself invisible, she bent her head, as each tear dropped onto the polished floor.

News traveled rapidly, and other students peered through their classroom doors and spoke in hushed whispers as Ela set out to walk the two-and-a-half-mile journey home. A day that started with normality and routine had turned into one of chaos and grief. At 11, Ela had the heartbreaking, unenviable task of announcing the death of our mother to the family.

Mom made our family complete. When we lost her, we lost the centerpiece to our lives – we lost that fundamental link that brought us together and made us whole. It would take many years before we could begin to come to terms with the devastating events of that day and reconnect the bonds of family identity and belonging. The absence of medical care, the struggles of making it through each day, and the relentless burdens of poverty and isolation in a remote village weighed heavily on our young shoulders.

In the aftermath of mom's passing, the village united in grief at the loss of a cherished friend, neighbor and family member. The void left by her departure seemed insurmountable; it was like a guillotine had fallen sharply to dismember our family's essence. It was the end of the old and familiar in our short lives. It was a moment that threw us into the abyss of the unknown, and we would be confronted with the stark realities of life.

During the week of my mother's passing, our little home overflowed as neighbors and friends arrived with food and condolences. Everyone came together to remember my beloved mother and comfort one another at her loss. However, Ela was inconsolable; her grief was laid bare and her sobs could be heard through the chattering noises in our crowded house.

Over the years, when I have reflected on that day, I sometimes wondered if Ela's tears were not only fueled by the devastation of losing our mother, but a combination of that grief and the overwhelming reality of being the eldest child and feeling a weight of new responsibilities at a young age. My own 5-year-old mind was completely bewildered. I couldn't quite come to grips with the fact that mom would never return. I hopelessly sought comfort among the sea of mourners, but there was no one that could provide me the support I desperately required.

My mother's body was transported back to Krasnopol by car, in a closed coffin provided by the hospital. Our family didn't have sufficient funds to pay for a funeral, so that became the responsibility of the government. State officials facilitated a simple burial, but would not allow mourners – not even my father or Helena, my grandmother – to attend.

When we are born, we are brought to the church for baptism to be welcomed into the faith. Practicing Catholics attend mass each Sunday, donning their best clothes to give praise and thanks. When we die, we are brought to the church to be welcomed into the afterlife. Catholic funerals hold a special place in the religion. The rituals around death and dying become part of the grieving process, providing comfort and solace for the bereaved. My mother received no such funeral, and this heartless omission only served to exacerbate the loss and confusion surrounding mom's death.

In what should have been a relatively simple procedure, the abysmal health care offered by an autocratic government had led to the early death of my mother. Many years later, I learned that it was a burst gallbladder that had caused her demise on the operation table. In communist Poland, her death was officially classified as caused by an infectious disease. That determination resulted in the closed coffin, which prevented her family one last glimpse of a loved family member and did not allow the process of grieving to begin.

Even as an innocent 5-year-old, deep within my being, I believed that my father bore some responsibility for my mother's illness and ultimate death. Had he been a less selfish, self-absorbed man, he would have insisted that she seek medical attention when – day after day – she struggled to get out of bed because of her intense pain. If the cause of her pain had been diagnosed early enough, she would have had a much greater chance of survival. But by the time she was admitted to hospital, it was most likely too late.

In the immediate aftermath of my mother's death, what was an already strained relationship between my grandma and my father intensified. There were constant arguments and disagreements, often about mundane matters. And then, just days after the funeral, my father walked out on his family to the home of the woman who would become his second wife. He departed with a small parcel of clothes and personal items under his arm, without so much as a goodbye; without any word of comfort, or love, or regret.

Grandmother, Ela, Teresa, Krysia and Asia

We were left under the care of our grandmother, dramatically shifting the family dynamic. Grandma was 60 years old at the time, and already beaten down by years of grueling manual work on the farm. With no male in the family to do the physical work necessary to keep the farm productive and maintain some level of financial stability, it became impossible for her to continue to care for four young children. We went from being a typical farming family in northeast Poland, with a comfortable humdrum existence where nothing much ever happened, to waking one morning and finding our lives demolished by a wrecking ball. We were bruised, battered and emotionally traumatized. Henryk arrived from Krakow and Helena from Olecko for the gathering after my mother's funeral. Long after we went to bed, my grandmother, aunt and uncle stayed up – and in hushed tones, they discussed and agreed upon our future.

When my aunt and uncle left Krasne, they took my siblings with them. Henryk took Joanna, who was then just 9 months old, home to Krakow. Ela and Teresa left with Aunt Helena to join her already large brood. I would have thought my father would be involved in the negotiations; however, he showed as much interest in the welfare of his children as he would have about learning how to paint his fingernails.

Whatever the adjustments that came about in our lives, it was nothing in comparison to the abrupt transformation in my grandmother's circumstances. Within a few short days, she had lost her youngest precious daughter, not to mention my father's physical strength on the farm. She was left with the responsibility of raising a 5-year-old, traumatized by the loss of her mother and siblings. But without so much as a missed beat, Grandma picked up the pieces of her life. Her only comfort was her faith and church. I can never remember her ever complaining about the misfortune life had brought her at a time when she should have been able to take a back seat and let others take care of her.

So I remained with my grandmother in the village, and was consoled in some small way by the familiarity of the only home I had ever known. The farm had once been the center of our family life; and while being around Grandma provided sustenance, my 5-year-old self was confused. I found it difficult to process the pronounced similarities between her and my mom, who had possessed so many of grandma's traits. My grandma also provided a constant reminder of my previous life and the acute absence of my mother and siblings.

I often think about the weight of responsibility that was placed on my young shoulders. I tried to help my grandmother with the chores, assisting her around the house and tending to the farm, and emulating her actions. I very much felt the absence of my sisters – especially Ela, who had so frequently filled a motherly role when Mom and Grandma were working in the fields. Ela and I had a special bond. Although she was only 37 miles away, in Suwalki, it seemed like the other side of the world to my young self. There would be, however, several occasions over the ensuing years when Ela would overcome the obstacles and the cost of travel to take a bus from Suwalki to Krasnopol to see me.

Whenever I was told that Ela was coming, I would take off, walking two hours through the fields to greet her at the bus stop. I lived for those visits, although they inevitably brought me further grief; I would be inconsolable when she departed again.

Joanna was still a baby when she was taken to Krakow by Uncle Henryk, and I rarely saw her. Henryk and his wife already had a toddler, so Joanna's fostering with them seemed like the natural choice. She would have a playmate near her own age.

I can recall one occasion when Uncle Henryk came to visit with his wife and Joanna. Joanna was only about 3 years old at the time, and I took her walking around the village, leaving Grandma, Henryk, and his wife Wanda to catch up. It was the 1960s, when it was believed that children should be seen and not heard – and certainly, they would not be part of a conversation among adults. The land around the village was mainly pasture, and I wanted to show Joanna around, so we went exploring. We came to a field and climbed the fence, only to find ourselves standing in the middle of a field confronted by a single, enormous bull. The bull was probably three or four times Joanna's height.

Joanna by this time was a city child, unfamiliar with vast sweeping fields and the prospect of a monstrous animal eyeing us as intruders. She began to cry uncontrollably with fear. I remember turning to her – and in a voice of absolute authority and calm, belying my own terror, said, "Don't you worry. I'm here to protect you." I grabbed her hand as we scrambled toward the fence and our escape route. We managed to exit the field unscathed and made our way back to Grandma's house.

That visit was short, and it would be many years before Joanna and I would see each other again. Uncle Henryk and Wanda were parents of a growing son and perhaps Henryk felt that having Joanna in the house would be beneficial for all. But once she reached her seventh birthday and was expected to start school, Uncle Henryk decided that it would be better for Joanna to return to the village and her grandmother. Joanna would live with us and help with the household until our grandmother passed away.

My grandmother was gifted with a caring and gentle nature, and her dedication to my well-being created a stronger bond between us. She was my anchor and the only certainty in my life. I had a great admiration for her; she was an exceptional role model and she had such a positive influence on me. Her slender frame belied an immense strength and a spirit that never faltered. She attracted people to her with understated wisdom and an ability to listen without judgment. Her demeanor and disposition was such that she was frequently sought out by others in the village for advice. I relished the hours I spent listening to her talk with older neighbors, savoring their stories and experiences.

Our lives and those of others in our community were consumed with a struggle for daily survival. It did not matter how hard we worked. There were never surplus funds and there was no such thing as a treat, however small. Grandma's desperation was evident when she spent days in the forest foraging for medicinal herbs. She gathered them and brought them home, turning them into poultices and cures for ailing neighbors. Nevertheless, her efforts earned her meager compensation. I think it was at that time in my life when I became aware that money brought choice and freedom – things that were lacking in our lives. Later, the fear of returning to those desolate days of crushing poverty provided me with the necessary drive and ambition to succeed. Those motivational factors would remain with me throughout my life.

The only area where we weren't lacking was our meals – because of my grandmother's excellent culinary skills. Her mastery of traditional Polish dishes was legendary in the community and she produced dishes of *pierogi* (dumplings made by wrapping unleavened dough around a filling and cooking in boiling water), *nalesniki* (crepes with different, often sweet, fillings), and nourishing, delicious soups. As a young girl, I had all the nourishment I needed to grow up fit and healthy. Hunger, thankfully, wasn't an issue.

Every week on Sunday, we undertook the two-hour journey by foot along a dirt road that skirted the lake to the church in Krasnopol. Of course, walking to the church was a more frequent event during Lent or periods of "devotions" and novenas. At those times, a particular saint would be prayed to if a family member had some special need, such as an illness where they sought a cure. Our commitment to going to church on Sunday was matched only by the devotion my grandmother had for her religion.

I spent a lot of time with Grandma when she would walk through the village. We were practically joined at the hip – everyone knew I was orphaned and what had happened to my mom. If I arrived home when Grandma was off in the forest or trying to sell produce in the market, I would call at our next door neighbor's house and play with my friend Jagoda. Although a few years older than me, Jagoda was my best friend, and her mom was always happy to see me come through the door. They always made me feel welcome. I was entertained – and often fed – by them until Grandma arrived home. She always knew that she would find me with the neighbors.

Christmas was a very special season. Not only would we celebrate the birth of Christ, but we would also commemorate Advent, which started at the beginning of December. The house was always decorated to welcome the birth of Jesus; and the pine forest, about a half mile behind the side of our home, provided beautiful natural Christmas trees. We would decorate them with simple candles, lighted ceremoniously in the evenings. I'm not so sure that any fire department on the planet would think it is a good idea to light candles on a tree, but fortunately we never had an accident. I have no recollection of any family in the village burning their house down because of the candles. Christmastime also meant that the scent of my grandmother's delicious baking would fill the house, as she would cook some of our favorite traditional dishes for the occasion.

In the quiet hours of winter evenings, we would sit beside the stove and talk. Grandma would pull up a chair, and she would sew or knit during the conversation – her hands were never idle. She would speak about all sorts of things: the family, the farm, the neighbors, her time in France before the war. Sometimes, she would speak about America. For so many Polish people, the United States was the Holy Grail, a land of freedom and an opportunity for a better life. Our lives offered little or no opportunities or freedom; indeed, the only things offered by communism in abundance were poverty, fear and terror. My imagination was piqued by grandmother's stories of the land called America, so far away. I was intrigued to find out what lay beyond my familiar surroundings and the Iron Curtain.

My mother's sister, Aunt Helena, knew of a Polish family whose son had emigrated to the United States. There, he met and married an American woman. The couple, Adolph and Anna, had no children, which they desperately wanted, so they decided to opt for the next best thing – adoption.

Aunt Helena, in conversation with Adolph's family, mentioned her sister's death and the orphans left behind. As four young children with no mother and an absent father, we presented the ideal opportunity for this couple who were interested in adopting a child. I was 8 years old when, one early spring morning, Adolph – then a total stranger – approached me as I walked through the village. Out of the blue, he stopped me and asked if I wanted to go to America.

It never occurred to me to ask how he knew who I was, or of my situation. In my innocence, I felt this stranger was my destiny. His interest in me confirmed all the stories that my grandmother had so often told me about America. I felt like the luckiest girl in my country; here was a man who was offering me a chance to build a decent life for my family and myself.

I believed that it was my life's dream – to be able to go to America and pave the way for a better life outside Poland and the Soviet Union. My greatest wish was to be able to send warmer clothes home to ensure my family would never have to feel cold again. As soon as the conversation finished with this stranger, I rushed home with one mission – to convince Grandma that going to America was my fate. The other side of the world was calling to me, and I was convinced that it was something I had to do.

For the first time in my eight years on the earth, I had a sense of optimism about my future. The prospect of adoption filled me with such excitement as I mentally prepared myself for the path that lay ahead.

I had already started school in the village, and was one of a dozen pupils in a small purpose-built school that taught grades one to four. Maybe it was the early trauma in my life that made me feel an outsider among my peers; I was constantly looking for ways to fit in and make friends. Perhaps I tried a bit too hard. I noticed that the other pupils in the class used their right hand when learning to write; I gravitated toward using my left hand. But using my left hand made me feel even more excluded and different, so I would spend hours at home practicing writing with my right hand, in my attempt to blend in.

I naively believed that my school peers would be pleased at my good luck in moving to America when I announced it in class one day. I could not have been more wrong. They resented my good fortune, and without any subtlety, they let me know it.

The adoption required my birth father's consent for a legal adoption, which was processed through the government prior to permission to leave the country. My grandmother wanted everything in order and legally secured before she would allow me to leave home. But with so much bureaucracy to weave her way through, the date of my departure was postponed. That led to me being teased at school, as the children in my class accused me of fantasizing this shining new future. They dismissed me as a dreamer, poking fun at my aspirations. However, they had no idea of my firm resolve. This was my destiny. I believed that my departure would reduce the burden on my grandmother, who had to take responsibility to care for me when she had already raised her own family.

In my naivete, I thought that an idyllic future lay ahead of me with a happy family life. I would have both a mom and dad, and I would be in a position where I could help my beloved grandma. I so much wanted to buy her some warm clothes, especially socks; she had dreadful trouble with cold feet that she could never seem to warm. I really wanted to send her socks so she wouldn't continue to suffer. Each morning after waking up, I would count down the days before I could step out into the unknown and truly begin this momentous adventure that was destined to be my life.

As a child being raised by a grandmother (albeit a loving and caring inspirational figure), I was different from all the other kids around me. By that time, the visual memory of my mother was becoming more vague, almost like a photograph left to fade in the summer sun. And I was mildly aware that after a while, the separation from Grandma would likewise cause the image of her beautiful face to fade in my mind.

At an early stage in the adoption process, I decided I needed to commit my home address in Krasne to memory, so if anything untoward happened, I could find my way back. Still, the prospect of adoption offered the possibility of being part of a family again. I could feel like a regular child, with two loving parents who were happy to embrace me as their own. That is what excited me, what I craved. I wanted to be able to talk with friends about what Mom and Dad were doing – I wanted that elusive membership as part of a family unit, under one roof, with the love of a mother and father.

Initially arranged for the summer of 1964, the departure to America was rescheduled to November. During those last summer months, I spent most of my time with my grandmother, rarely leaving her side. We tended to the farm, silently working in unison; and I continued helping her with the chores around the house. With fall in its dying days and the cusp of winter fast approaching, we worked hard. We had to ensure that the harvest was gathered and its yield was preserved, so my grandmother would have reserves to see her through the harshest months.

Grandmother had scraped together some money to buy material, cutting and stitching a new dress for my arrival in America; she wanted me to make an impression. I was to travel light with just one second-hand suitcase – acquired, most likely, from a neighbor – that was filled mostly with food and gifts for my new family. It was a gesture of gratitude; the gifts were to reassure my new family that we appreciated their gesture to adopt me and that we came from respectable stock.

Finally, the day arrived. I woke early to assist Grandma with the routine farm chores; I was determined to contribute as much as possible before my departure. Prior to leaving, I had never spent a single night outside our home in Krasne – it was the only home I had ever known.

It was Uncle Marian, Aunt Helena's husband, who picked me up and delivered me on the first stage of my journey. Ela, who was then 15 years old, was brought along to say goodbye. I experienced a real clash of emotions. On the one hand, I felt a dizzying excitement because of the impending adventure; but there was also an overwhelming awareness that I was leaving behind the people with whom I was closest – Grandma and Ela. In the hours prior to my departure, there was an ocean of tears from our small family gathering. Those tears cascaded into the very essence of our humble home.

I had no premonition of the type of future that lay ahead of me, but perhaps my grandmother's wisdom had transferred into my DNA as through osmosis when I made that decision to implant my home address into the core of my brain. While my departure caused me to feel a great sadness, I held no fear. The innocence of childhood carried me on the wings of hope to face my extraordinary adventure. However, if I knew then what I know now, I do not think I would have ever left. Grandma decided to stay behind, most likely because she was too upset. Before I left the house, she smothered me with one last embrace, and begged me to keep in touch and to write often. I left with the promise that I would never forget her or my mother and I would be a good daughter to my new parents. I told her that I would write to her frequently.

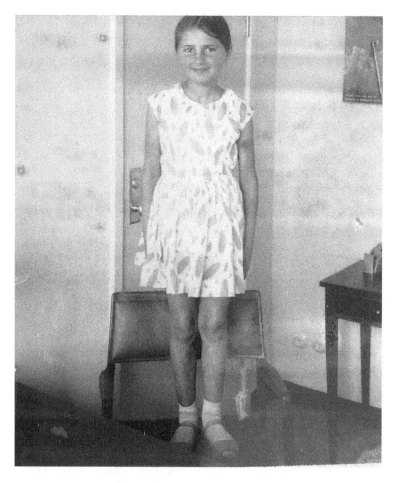

Day of departure from Poland to New York

The journey began with Ela and Uncle Marian carrying my suitcase, escorting me as we walked to Krasnopol to catch the train to Suwalki. Ela accompanied us onto the train to wait for its departure. As we sat together, crying and hugging, she pleaded with me to remember her Polish family and write as soon as I arrived. Ela became distraught when the screech of the whistle reverberated through the station to signal the train's imminent departure. I think it brought back memories of another member of her precious family that was lost to her. I pressed my face to the window to catch one last glimpse of Ela as the train pulled out of the station, and I remained that way for the longest time. I could feel the train pulling us farther apart with each mile.

We headed to Warsaw, my last stop in Poland before taking to the skies and another life. Other than the memorable visit to the dentist with my mom so many years before, the furthest I had traveled out of my village had been for school and to attend church in Krasnopol. When we traveled through Warsaw to the airport, it was my first time in a real city. The sheer size of the buildings, the paved roads and sidewalks, were mind-blowing. There were so many streets and so few trees or fields, not to mention the sheer number of people rushing around like ants on the march. It was my first time experiencing anything like that – and I was so excited. I was going to travel across Europe and on to America on a plane, something I had never even seen up close before. When we arrived at the airport, my uncle guided me through check-in and passport control before handing me over to the responsibility of the airline. I was provided with a pouch that hung around my neck, indicating that I was underage and required to be chaperoned. A stewardess was assigned to me to ensure I arrived safely.

The stewardess escorted me onto the plane, where she led me to my seat beside the window. I was filled with nervous excitement as we taxied down the runway. The engines roared and we picked up speed for takeoff. Feeling the velocity of the aircraft pushing us forward as we climbed into the skies, I felt as if my tummy had hit my spine. My heart was beating so hard that I thought it was going to jump out of my chest.

I looked out the window and gazed at the country of my birth as we soared higher and higher. Thes enormous landscape soon became the size of a small picture as we climbed above the clouds. After a short time, there was no more land visible. I have little recollection of much else about the flight except the stopover in Greenland, which was mesmerizing. In 1964, it wasn't possible to fly such a distance without making a stopover. So after many hours on the plane, we stopped for refueling in Greenland – a country that reflected its name, as all I could observe from above was vast swathes of greenery as far as the eye could see.

Philadelphia

When I arrived in the United States of America, it was just 12 months after the assassination of John F. Kennedy. We landed at the airport in New York that had been renamed to honor the Irish-American president, the descendant of immigrants. The stewardess who had the responsibility for me brought me through customs and passport control… and then promptly left me to my own devices. I think that her job was to hand me over to the safety of my adopted family, but she abandoned me once we cleared customs. She must have believed she had dealt with her responsibility at that point, and that her job was complete.

All the other passengers from the Polish flight had picked up their luggage. I watched them come into the arrival hall and greet waiting family members. There were hugs, tears of joy, and sometimes whoops of excitement. I was a vulnerable child looking on at these scenes, sitting alone.

It dawned on me that for the first time in my life, I was completely and utterly on my own. I was at my wits' end; as I scanned the scene, panic rose in me. I was clutching my throat so tightly that I was unable to breathe properly.

I was no longer in a village where I knew every nook and cranny like the back of my hand, but in a strange city and a strange land. I struggled to understand what was going on; everyone was speaking a language I was hearing for the first time. There was no one waiting for me – no one with a smile on their face or holding my name written on a piece of paper. I simply could not communicate. I knew I was well beyond the point of no return and I was also aware that failure was not an option. I had come too far to give up, and as the minutes passed, I held onto the belief that everything would work out somehow.

I was left sitting for what seemed like hours. Eventually, the stranger who approached me in Krasne that day appeared; he introduced himself as my new father. Without offering to take my hand for reassurance, he picked up my suitcase and began walking at a fast pace. I had to run behind him to keep up as we headed for the parking lot. His car was enormous compared to anything I had seen in Poland, and we took off, heading out of JFK and straight towards my new hometown of Philadelphia.

I felt no jet lag. Adrenalin pumped through my veins; I was trying to absorb everything that was going on around me as we drove through the night. I was hypnotized by the sheer quantity of street lights in the towns and cities we passed through along the highway. Before this, I had seen so few cars in my life that the sight of these monstrous Cadillacs and Mustangs was mesmerizing. On top of that, there were enormous trucks moving down the roads with more lights than the average house in Poland. They illuminated the highways as they pushed through the dark night, taking goods from state to state. I was totally captivated by this young nation with its unbounding confidence, vibrancy, and limitless opportunities.

We stopped at a gas station to fill the tank and use the bathroom. For the first time in my life, I entered a fast-food restaurant – actually, I had never been on the inside of any restaurant before, fast-food or otherwise. But my new father didn't want to linger – we ate quickly and continued our journey.

It was well past midnight when we arrived in Philadelphia. We turned onto Grays Avenue and I got a glimpse of my new home. My new mother came to the door and introduced herself as I stepped inside. She took my suitcase, which contained all my possessions and documents, along with the gifts from my Polish family. I was shown to my bedroom; and while I had never seen a movie or heard of Disney yet, later on I would compare my humble home in Krasne to this new "luxury" – like something out of a Disney princess movie. My room was decorated in pink, and it felt enormous in comparison to what I was familiar with at home with Grandma.

In that moment I felt a compelling gratitude for the good fortune of having two loving parents in a beautiful modern home, the likes of which I had never imagined. To me, it signified a new beginning, the opportunity to create a new life. The time difference eventually caught up with me; I fell into a deep sleep and dreamed of my new family, feeling a real sense of belonging for the first time. I believed I was the luckiest girl in the world, finally finding a home. I was ready to begin my life anew, where I could grow and keep an open mind to every opportunity I would encounter.

After I woke up the next morning, I tried to absorb everything. I was pinching myself – it was like winning a lottery. I was excited to explore my new unfamiliar surroundings. My new mother seemed kind, but we had a language barrier; she didn't speak Polish, which made communication almost impossible. As we ate breakfast together, my new father acted as a translator for our conversation and all seemed to go reasonably well, every-thing considered.

However, I became uneasy when I realized that the dress I had worn on my trip was nowhere to be seen, along with each and every other item I had brought from Poland. As I walked through the house, I realized that one of the rooms was secured with a sturdy padlock. Even at such a young age, it set off alarm bells. My throat dried and I felt a chill traveling through my bones, sparking more than a tinge of fear. It slowly became evident that my entire Polish life and belongings were locked behind a door. I could never find out the reason for that, but my things were never to appear again.

At the time of my adoption, my adoptive father, Adolph, was 53; his wife Anna, an American of Italian descent, was 39. While my new father's family remained in Poland, Anna was his only relative in the US. They were a middle-lower class couple. Anna worked in the local hospital as a dietician, and Adolph worked as a mechanic for Boeing Aviation. What seemed like a Disney dream castle when I first arrived was, in reality, an average Philadelphia rowhouse with three bedrooms, one bathroom, and a small backyard.

My first week in these unfamiliar surroundings was very challenging. Once again, I felt that I was different; even after all my efforts, I was still an outsider trying my damndest to belong and be accepted. I wanted my new family to love me and tried everything I could think of to please them. I was desperate to fit in and assimilate.

I had only been in Philadelphia for two weeks when homesickness kicked in. An all-encompassing sadness enveloped me in waves; it was overwhelm-ing at times. There were occasions when it caught me like an unexpected gust of wind, and the tears would well up and flow at the most random moments. It felt as if my whole family had been wiped out in one blow – I was heartbroken. I could think of nothing else but how much I missed my family in Poland.

I asked my father if I could write to my grandmother to let her know I had arrived safely. He seemed supportive, and I penned a simple letter, assuring those I held most dear of my well-being and happiness with my new parents. However, in a subsequent letter a few weeks later, I expressed my feelings of isolation, loneliness and longing for my family. When my father picked up the letter and read it, his face went purple with rage. Shouting at me, he forbade me from ever contacting my family again. This man made it clear that I was never to talk about any of my relations in Poland to anyone; and if I disobeyed and he heard something through the grapevine, I would face his wrath. A few weeks later, another padlock went on the mailbox outside our house to prevent me from accessing any communication from Poland.

I found that everything in my life was controlled by this couple. In no uncertain terms, I was informed that my sole *raison d'être* was to wait on their needs and care for them into old age. My role was to be a servant in their household and these so-called parents were the masters of the home. It didn't take long before my dreams of a new life in America were shattered. I felt as though my life was turning into something akin to a horror movie. I had no one to turn to from the constant fear and sadness inflicted by this man who professed to be my dad – there was no one to comfort or reassure me.

My new mother tried very hard to communicate with me in those first few weeks after my arrival, but she made no attempt to provide me with English classes. My only way to try and make her understand what I needed was to point to things. It was a cause of great frustration for both of us; I was left feeling bewildered and frightened as I tried to make sense of it all.

Not only was I struggling with the language barrier, but I felt isolated, as if I was in solitary confinement in a prison – unable to communicate with a single soul except my adoptive Polish-speaking father.

While Adolph had no immediate family in the United States, Anna had a family – a sister, Viola, along with her husband and child. They lived just outside Philadelphia. During the first months after I arrived, we would often visit them over a weekend – perhaps once or twice a month.

It was an opportunity to get to know my cousins, and we would spend our time playing as the adults chatted and drank coffee in the kitchen. But I believe Viola did not approve of or like my father, and on one of the visits they had a falling out, which put an abrupt end to our get-togethers.

After that, my mother and father did not bother much with anyone outside the family. They never had visitors – no neighbors or friends came inside our home. They kept to themselves.

I still wonder if it was sheer frustration that caused my mother to begin physically abusing me. Maybe she was irritated at the language barrier, or perhaps her abuse was an attempt to appease her husband, who intimidated and oppressed her. Perhaps his actions toward her caused her to take her vexation and revenge out on me.

There were times when I had to wear long sleeves and pants to cover the bruising that covered my body. I endured the physical punishments in silence, never allowing my mother to see the pain she was inflicting on me. I was powerless to stop the vicious treatment, but I developed a steel determination never to let them see how much I was hurting – either physically or emotionally. I kept my tears for nighttime, using my pillow as a muffle so they couldn't hear me crying long into the night.

On one sunny summer Sunday morning, about six months after moving in with my new parents, I was up early. I was dressed in a T-shirt and shorts, and I wandered into their bedroom to ask a question, as would any 10-year-old daughter. They were getting ready for the day, and preparing to decide when they would go to church for mass. My mother left the room to go downstairs and organize breakfast; she hadn't even reached the bottom step when my father – without saying a word – walked over and ran his hand over the front of my body, lingering on my flat chest. My gut told me that there was something very wrong, as my body stiffened and I was seized with fear. I removed myself from his presence at the first opportunity.

For the remainder of the time I lived in that house, I never again walked across the threshold of their bedroom. Despite their united front, I suspect that my adoptive father isolated, dominated and subjugated my new mother. This woman was trapped in a coercive relationship, but it wasn't recognized as such then. It was not a topic that was discussed much or indeed even acknowledged in the 1960s.

Within a few days of arriving in Philadelphia, I was enrolled at St. Mary's of Czestochowa, a Polish Catholic elementary school, just a few blocks from home. In contrast to the 15-pupil school in Krasne, there were about 300 children in my new school. I had never experienced anything like it before. The schoolyard would fill with the students during breaks, with skipping ropes and games, shrieks, and screams. I would sit alone, watching it all.

Despite Poland being a Catholic country, education there was secular, with little religious influence. In Philadelphia, St. Mary's of Czestochowa was run by nuns – women I had never previously encountered. I was fascinated by the long black clothes and the wimples covering their hair, neck and part of their face. Their apparel seemed very strange to me. As for the students, we were required to wear a uniform – a white shirt, a blue skirt, and ugly blue shoes. Any expression of individuality or creativity within variations of the uniform was firmly discouraged.

First day in school with my adopted mother and teacher of another class

While I had few friends and walked alone to school on most days, the classroom did offer a much-needed escape from the loneliness I experienced in my new home. I looked forward to the respite, even if it was for just a few hours a day. However, going to school soon became almost as isolating as home. No one was assigned to show me around or familiarize me with my surroundings. Each day that I walked through the school gates, it felt as though I had been dropped off in the middle of an unknown city, left to find my own way.

For a 10-year-old, it was an intimidating situation, but it did not dampen my eagerness to make the most of the opportunity to learn. I desperately wanted to find my refuge in education, and I believed that being a good student was the way to succeed. However, yet another disappointment awaited me. I found that I was isolated in class due to my very limited English and heavy Polish accent. There was little interest or effort shown by my fourth-grade teacher, Sister Olga, in helping me to assimilate. I would like to think it was because she was already overburdened with work, and that taking on a child with no English would have been one task too many. However, my lack of English language skills succeeded in compounding my feeling of helplessness. It contributed to a lack of confidence and self-worth, especially when I was arbitrarily assigned a task to cover the schoolbooks for my peers in fourth grade. That menial task continued throughout my entire first year in school. I received no teaching and learned practically nothing in that first year; I fell behind academically. But my circumstances only served to increase my hunger for opportunity and knowledge, to prepare to escape from the awful situation I found myself in.

The language barriers created obstacles in making any close friendships with the other students. My inability to speak fluent English emphasized our differences, casting me as an outsider. While some of my classmates made token attempts to be friendly, many kept their distance, preferring – as many girls do – to stay within their own cliques. Each day I traveled to school alone, ate lunch in the dining hall with a few students, and remained frustrated and unsure of how to fit in or belong.

When I eventually made some friends, some would call my home; when they did, my parents' suspicious nature was off-putting for anyone to cross the threshold. My parents were loners, keeping to themselves, with no friends on the street. To the outside world, they were devout Catholics, regular mass-goers and the type of people who sat in the front of the church so others could see them.

However, their outward display of devout Catholicism did not mirror their behavior behind closed doors. I found their whole charade difficult to reconcile; my adoptive father was the embodiment of house devil and street angel. Their contradictory behavior not only left me questioning the sincerity of the religious faith of others, but also cast a shadow over my own belief in God's love and the goodness of humanity. The duality of my parents' conduct shattered my trust, leaving me wary of the world around me. However, while I sometimes think that they stole my innocence, they also didn't realize that their malice instilled an independent nature within me. Their behavior led me to resolve to forge a better life for myself; and I was determined to never forget my family in Poland or my commitment to help them.

It took about a year before my school life significantly improved. Eventually, I was able to communicate, and I began to create a small circle of friends. A girl named Terry and I became friends in school once I learned some English. She was my own age and had a Polish background too, so she had some understanding of my mindset and background. She lived just three blocks away and we were in the same class. We would sometimes walk to school together and she would invite me to her house after school. Terry was one of the few friends who would come over to my house as well, and her friendship was the catalyst for my acceptance among our peers. As our friendship developed, I eventually began to feel like a normal person in my new environment.

In the two years since my arrival in the United States, I had grown several inches. On the verge of puberty at 11 years old, my height belied my young age. My father began taking me to Schuylkill Park, a well-known spot in Philadelphia about a 20 minute drive from our home. It was somewhat unusual for him to show any affection or provide something akin to a treat, but I did not think to question his motivation for this indulgence. When we arrived, I was overjoyed to see green spaces and an abundance of trees. The park brought memories of my home in Poland and reminded me of the serenity that can be found in nature's beauty.

True to form, my father's behavior at the park soon took a turn, and his warped motivation became obvious. At first I thought he was playing games with me, and I was puzzled when he began to run and disappear among the trees or hunker behind the park benches. The first time it happened, I was left standing, jaw dropped in surprise. I turned full circle, on the verge of panic, to see where he went. It took me some time to realize the disturbing motivation behind his actions; I believe he wanted me to be harmed, attacked by strangers, so he could justify the abuse he inflicted on me at home. If I had been attacked, he would justify the beating as a means of controlling me, to keep me "safe." This realization left me both terrified and traumatized.

What I thought would be a place of joy and refuge became a dark, petrifying place where I felt unsafe; I could be prey for any deviant who happened to cross my path. I would keep my head down, staring at the ground, fearful of making eye contact. I avoided any interaction to prevent retaliation. My feeling of isolation and loneliness was compounded and complete. I had no adult in the world who would look out for me and there was no one I could turn to; I was not even aware I had rights. My parents ensured that every aspect of my life was completely under their control, and I lived in absolute fear – fear of my parents, fear of strangers, fear of contacting my family in Poland, and even fear of returning to Poland into a completely unknown situation.

Night after night as I lay in bed, I would look out at the moon. It was the only time I felt some connection to my family on the other side of the world. I knew that it was the same moon they could see, and in my mind I would imagine the oceans that separated us dissolving, shrinking the endless miles and reuniting us in spirit. It may have been a frivolous idea, but it was the only way I could survive – imagining a connection with the only people who ever truly loved me.

During my first few years in America, bedtime was an opportunity to release the grief from the pressure cooker of physical and emotional pain inflicted on me each day. I would cry myself to sleep every night, hidden under the covers. But time passed, and after five long years of crying, I stopped shedding tears. I made a decision that crying was not getting me where I wanted to be, and I would no longer use tears as an outlet for my emotions. I buried my feelings deep inside and replaced my tears with a stoic silence. It was an act of defiance against my torturers.

We did not have Thanksgiving in Poland, so for my first few years in the States, the holiday meant little to me. However, it was Christmas that brought back painfully sweet memories of times with my grandma, with neighbors helping us to haul the pine tree home from the forest for decoration. A Christmas gift would be something Grandma crafted for me – a knitted sweater or hat, or a new dress sewn with her own hands. There had been no mention of St. Nicholas or Father Christmas in Communist Poland, and I was ignorant of Santa's ability to fly all over the world in 24 hours, gifting toys to middle-class children across the free world.

The holiday in my new life provided a stark contrast to how Christmas had been in Poland, and I often think that Thanksgiving and Christmas can be a challenging time for many people. There is an expectation – endorsed by advertising – that these holidays are occasions for celebratory family reunions, filled with happiness and joy for everyone. Despite the hype, we are not homogenous, and each of our paths can throw up a very different narrative. For many of us, it's not a happy one.

The atmosphere at home with my adopted parents was even more strained than usual during the holiday period. The decorations were taken down from the attic each Christmas and a pine tree was purchased. I knew that most kids went along with their parents to pick out a tree, but that never happened in our home. My father would arrive home with the tree on the roof of the car and then unceremoniously dump it in the hallway. The fairy lights never worked, and he would spend hours trying to figure out which light had the dodgy bulb that prevented the whole set from working. The house was duly decorated, outside and in. A crib representing the birth of baby Jesus with the Holy Family was on display in the hallway, and the large tree was adorned with flashing lights – once my father got them working again. Time spent at home was a challenge during the best of times, so there was palpable tension when we pretended that we were all loving and happy in the season of giving.

We attended Midnight Mass on Christmas Eve together, all of us wearing new clothes that were bought for the occasion. My father would march us up to the top of the church so we could be perceived by neighbors as a devout family. Older teenagers would congregate at the back of the church, coming in after spending a few hours in the local bar. A second priest would be sent down to the back of the church to act as a doorman and throw out any one who showed up drunk.

On Christmas morning after breakfast, we would unwrap our presents from under the tree. My parents had little imagination as to what gifts would be suitable for a young girl, but I would pretend that the gifts were exactly what I wished for. Beyond the strained smiles and pretense of delight with the gifts, my father's undercurrent of anger simmered – always on the verge of exploding into an absolute volcanic rage.

My parents liked people to think we were a close-knit, loving family, doing normal things like exchanging gifts. However, the temporary joy of each Christmas season would soon be overshadowed by my parents taking each and every gift back. It was a painful reminder of their underlying control and manipulation. Initially, I blamed myself, wondering what I had done wrong to warrant such actions. However, as the pattern persisted year after year, I began to see the truth: it was a deliberate tactic to hurt and to assert dominance. Despite the hurt, the now-familiar routine of school, along with the support of some friends, became my refuge and sanctuary. It was a place where I could regain a sense of normalcy and stability.

There was a notion pushed by the United States media after World War II that Polish people were intellectually inferior. This notion was probably motivated by the media's anti-communist stance, and attempts to "other" people who were different. That narrative lingered well into the 1960s; Poles were frequently ridiculed for their accents and were the butt of many jokes. The attitudes towards Polish people led me to experience many challenges when trying to form friendships. The girls in my neighborhood kept their distance, despite every effort on my part to reach out.

Even after several years, I was not fully accepted. I did not completely fit in, remaining an aberration – an outsider. Summer vacations brought their own trials. Without many friends with whom to hang out, I would walk the 15 blocks to the public swimming pool and spend my days alone, watching other families and friends gathering for fun days. I had a neighbor, Dorothy, who was a similar age and went to the school across from our house; but my efforts to reach out were rebuffed, and her clique of friends seemed impregnable. I resorted to forming friendships with her younger sisters, Angela and Lisa. However, our age difference made it difficult to form a strong bond.

By the time I was 12 years old, I had come to an adult decision – I would make it my life's goal to find a job that provided me with financial stability and a pension for my retirement. Memories of my grandmother's life and the hardship she endured haunted me. I realized that she was trapped in poverty from which she could not escape. The physical work and effort she expended just to put food on the table ravaged her body; she endured it all without any security or safety net, and without a whisper of complaint. Grandma relied solely on herself. And after three years of living in the United States, I recognized that I was the only person I could depend on to direct the course of my future. I had to take control and make all the right decisions that would provide the necessary security that was so elusive to this point.

On my street, Grays Avenue, Philadelphia

Finally, as my English improved and I shook off my heavy Polish accent, I began to be more accepted. I acquired a circle of friends. I had finished St. Mary's of Czestochowa Elementary School and moved on to West Catholic Girls High School, which entailed a bus trip each day. The school fee was $400 per year (quite a sum in those days); so, after my first year in high school, my adoptive parents informed me they had arranged for me to move to a public school where education was free.

While the nuns in West Catholic High were very strict, they provided an excellent education. So, I was determined to stay in the same school – and I had a plan. I was a growing 15-year-old by that time, and at a gangly 5 feet, 8½ inches, I looked a little older than my years. The legal minimum age for work was 16, so I knew I required a job that paid cash and would not go through the Internal Revenue Service. While browsing the local Philadelphia newspaper one day, I came across a modeling agency advertisement, seeking girls for work. I didn't hesitate. I knew I was tall and thin enough to take on the work; and the next day, I turned up at the agency's office.

My height and figure made me a popular choice for runway work. One time, I ended up modeling most of the clothes in a show – the clothes fit me better than any of the other girls. The money I earned went toward my education. And despite my young years, my parents had no issue with me working. My income would save them the cost of paying for my school fees that year. Later, I found a job distributing American Express applications to students at colleges and universities, which paid me for each applicant I signed up.

Landing jobs to pay for my education was not the only plan I had in mind. While other juniors and seniors at West Catholic High embraced college prep classes, I decided on a different path. I made the difficult choice to forgo a traditional college education. Considering that my parents were not subsidizing my high school education, I knew they were hardly going to support several years of college. But West Catholic High had a program that allowed me to attend school in the mornings and work in the afternoons. It was not the standard formula for success that the school advocated; but it offered students like me an opportunity to gain meaningful employment through certificates in shorthand and typing. It felt like something I needed to do in order to provide myself with employable skills.

I had the stamina and the grades to go to college, but my unconventional decision was guided by life's lessons in logic and self-reliance. Given my chaotic and traumatic experiences, not to mention the lack of a support system, college seemed like another mountain to climb. I was in a hurry to get out, get working and – most importantly – succeed. I had weathered many storms that forged my ambition. I was an independent spirit, unable and unwilling to rely on others to take care of my future or my needs.

So, after my regular morning classes, I stepped out into the workforce each afternoon, embracing a role as a receptionist in a parcel delivery business. The business resembled the early days of Amazon, albeit on a microscopic scale. The long hours and weekends I sacrificed were an investment in myself, and my work allowed me to save money for my education, take out a loan for my first car, and indulge in small luxuries like decent clothes and makeup.

The physical punishment at home continued, with brutal and unprovoked beatings. On occasion, I would call out my father on his behavior in order to preserve some shred of dignity on my part – but mostly, that would just increase his level of anger. He would beat me so severely that I would be left with welts on my legs and arms. This tormentor who called himself my father saw my punishment as a way to assert his dominance and control me into submission.

We had an old-fashioned desktop telephone at home – the kind with a rotary dial – that probably weighed a couple of pounds. I was in my mid-teens; I had done something innocuous, but it annoyed my father and sent him into a blind rage. In a totally unprovoked and unexpected swift move, he grabbed the phone and hit me over the head with it. It stunned me, and as I collapsed on the floor I fell into a semi-conscious state. His action was so unexpected and sudden that I found myself in acute shock. I was unable to scream or fight back.

Once I was on the ground, both my parents began kicking me – they were in a frenzy of hate and anger. They were kicking every part of my body as I lay in a fetal position, trying to protect myself with my hands over my head. They kicked me from one room to another, eventually kicking me onto the porch, and finally onto the street. It took some time before I could even try to pick myself up from the ground. Every inch of my body was wracked with pain, and my face and my T-shirt were covered in blood. When I did eventually manage to stand on my feet, the blood had dried. I began walking aimlessly around the streets in a dazed state, without any idea of where I was going.

A girl from the neighborhood saw me wandering; and when she realized that I had experienced severe trauma, she convinced me to come back to her house. She helped me clean up, and ensured that I was hydrated. She almost poured water into me. But when I left her house, I continued to wander for several more hours – walking the streets, trying to figure out just what had provoked the attack and what I had said that was so wrong.

I wanted to leave. I was miserable and afraid for my life. I agonized over the consequences, but eventually decided to return to the house of pain and not report the incident to the police. My reason for staying silent was a gnawing fear of ending up in a foster home. Having heard several horror stories about foster parents, I reasoned that there was no point in jumping from one terrible situation into something similar or even worse. It was best to stick to what was familiar, I thought, and so I eventually found my way back. I arrived home late into the night and my father was in the living room. Without exchanging any words or acknowledging his presence, I climbed the stairs and went up to my room to sleep.

The beatings became so frequent that my life became unbearable. I could see no way out of the desolation and fear that was literally being knocked into me. I never knew what was going to trigger another hammering. I questioned why God had allowed this cruelty to happen to me. What did I do wrong to deserve such an abusive family? All I wanted was to be loved and to please my parents, but there was nothing on the planet I could do to make this evil man and woman happy. He used his power to try and demoralize me – an orphaned child who had done nothing wrong. This man wanted me to submit to him, and I suspect he would have eventually sexually assaulted me. But I was resolute – I was never going to surrender to him.

In my teens, I was assimilating into American culture and society more and more. Each year the local church in our neighborhood, Our Lady of Loreto, held a summer carnival for the parishioners. They would close the street and set up stalls, selling cotton candy and toffee apples along with rides for the kids. I met Kathy and her sister Patty on one of those occasions. Kathy was about my age and went to another school in the parish. The sisters were part of a large family of six kids, whose mother was constantly stressed with money worries.

Kathy and I hit it off immediately; she had a wicked sense of humor and always made me laugh. She was my beacon of hope and became my closest friend. We were inseparable in our teenage years. Kathy was someone I could speak to, and share my worries and my hopes of reuniting with my family in Poland.

I was also lucky to have made friends with Terry in grade school and then with Beth in high school. Terry was also of Polish heritage and we were in the same class. Terry introduced me to Beth, and we three girls were all very tall for our age. Very few boys our own age could look us in the eye – we towered over many of them. When we hooked up to go out on a weekend, we were a sight to behold – almost like Amazonian warriors. A guy would have had to be very confident to approach any one of us on a night out. With these new friends and my increasing confidence, the physical abuse at home seemed to become less frequent, but a more disturbing shift occurred. My father began giving off bad vibes, looking at me in an increasingly menacing manner. His manner shifted from that of a father (albeit an abusive, bullying father) toward a young daughter, to a realization that I was blossoming into a young woman.

I could feel his eyes following me around the room, scrutinizing my every move; and I have no doubt that it didn't escape my adopted mother's notice either. I felt uncomfortable and threatened in his presence, and wouldn't enter a room if he was there alone. He began making inappropriate comments and calling me hurtful names, often referring to me as a slut and a whore. He insinuated that I owed him for adopting me, and for saving me from a life of poverty and misery in Poland. He relished in demeaning and belittling me, using crude, cruel words to manipulate and control my actions. This man did his best to crush any confidence that I was beginning to exhibit. He wanted to dominate me absolutely, so I would be totally reliant on him and unable to live an independent life.

My adoptive mother remained a passive onlooker, never standing up to the brute. Sometimes, she joined him in spewing out verbal abuse. I suspect that she was also a victim of his bullying; perhaps her joining in was a tactic she developed as her only means to have her husband on her side.

One evening, my mother went out to go to the movies with one of her few friends. She had not even pulled out of the driveway when my father began a vicious verbal assault – snarling and saying that I owed him. I was at the end of my tether. I was exhausted from constantly battling this man who made me feel as if I was taking up space on the planet and undeserving of any affection or love. I could see no way out of my nightmare; I felt the only option left to me was to end the misery and take my own life.

After my father left the room and went upstairs, I went to the kitchen and filled a large glass of water. It was possibly a subconscious decision, but I had no plan in mind the previous week when I had purchased some over-the-counter sedatives. Along with the sedatives, there were other pills in the medicine cabinet, prescribed for my father to manage his pain after a car accident. The never-ending emotional distress I felt was so deep and without hope; I didn't hesitate. With a few gulps of water and a bottle of aspirin, I washed them all down.

As I lay on the couch in the living room, I could see my father watching me. He was sitting on the top step of the stairs. A tremendous feeling of peace washed over me. I gave in to my urge to call Kathy, to thank her for being my best friend and bringing some joy into my life. The drugs were acting much quicker than I expected, and Kathy detected the slur in my voice as I was passing out. She immediately realized the seriousness of the situation and alerted her parents, explaining that she suspected I had overdosed.

When her parents called the police, Kathy could not tell them my address. She knew where I lived, but we never needed to know each other's house numbers. There were police cars and an ambulance going up and down Grays Avenue, looking for my house. Eventually, Kathy's sister, Patty, and her father brought the ambulance over to my home. The response team broke down the door into the house, thinking I was alone; my father hadn't bothered to come downstairs. It was likely that he went into his bedroom so the response team didn't know he was home.

I recall the medics shaking me violently in an attempt to get me to come around. A neighbor later told me that as the response team brought me out of the house, I was sobbing; pleading with them to just leave me alone to die. I was taken to the hospital and remember waking up there with a doctor pounding on my chest. The medical team discharged me a few days later; I returned to the house of terror and my tormentors.

Strangely, not one single person in the hospital spoke to me about the events that had landed me there. I could only conclude that my father had invented some cock-and-bull story, and no one thought to question its veracity. During the ensuing two weeks, my parents behaved as normal parents should – but that was a short-lived experience, and the nightmare began to reoccur.

The suicide episode left me deflated; while I experienced a sense of deep sadness and hopelessness, I had no option but to snap out of it quickly. I realized that I required a long-term plan, not a short-term solution. I rationalized that even with the chaos and abuse, home remained the only stability in my life. I believed that going into the foster system would only lead to more pain. I felt strangely comforted by the consistency of my life; I liked knowing where I would sleep at night. This home – with these people – had to be my anchor. Losing a roof over my head would be losing myself entirely. No matter how dark and tumultuous my life had become, I could not allow that to happen.

Spreading Wings

Not having a lot of spare cash, I would go down to the mall and window-shop. I would imagine that I had the resources to dress in some of the beautiful clothes on display in the stores. I would use these trips as a way to dream, and also keep myself out of the house for a few extra hours. It was on one of those occasions – as I wandered from store to store – that a middle-aged man, looking every bit a businessman in a smart suit, approached me. He produced a business card, and with impeccable manners, introduced himself. He asked me if I was interested in entering a beauty contest. Since I had no arrangements to meet any of my friends that day, I took up the offer, thinking it would be fun and a new experience.

He gave me the phone number of the organizer, Mrs. Lee, and wrote down her home address. One phone call later, and I was on a bus to see Mrs. Lee in her rowhouse in South Philadelphia. When the door opened, I was greeted by a middle-aged, motherly-type lady. She welcomed me warmly as she escorted me into her living room and offered me a seat. After she went to the kitchen to make some coffee, she reappeared with a tray of coffee and cookies; she made small talk to help me feel at ease.

Mrs. Lee was organizing the beauty contest as a fundraiser for a chapter of the Knights of Columbus, a charitable, traditional conservative Catholic organization with more than a million male members around the globe. She talked me through the process of the contest, explaining that it was to take place the following week.

I was excited at the prospect of participating in such a glamorous event. She advised me that I needed two outfits – a bathing suit and an evening gown, one for each of the two competitions on the evening of the event. It was late fall; and in those days, there were no bathing suits to be found for sale during that season in any store in Philadelphia. Bathing suits could only be found on sale during the summer months. Mrs. Lee was kind enough to offer to loan me a bathing suit, and I was able to purchase a simple, elegant purple dress in one of the larger department stores.

The contest would be held in an upscale hotel in the city – and as the day of the event came around, I was giddy with anticipation and excitement. Soon after I arrived at the venue, the room began filling up. As the audience and guests arrived, the chatter became louder; people were greeting each other and finding their seats. A lot of the girls had brought family along to support them on their big night, but as with so many other events in my life, I was flying solo. I had informed my parents about the contest; but as I expected, they showed no interest in attending the function or supporting me.

Behind the scenes, there was organized chaos – all the girls were high on excitement and nerves. I applied my makeup and changed into my bathing costume, and I took my place in a line with the other contestants. As the lights dimmed and the music came up, I began to walk the runway. It was almost as if the low lighting threw a switch of confidence inside me, and I practically hovered above the runway, smiling and sashaying to the music. It was such a wonderful departure from my difficult home life, and I welcomed the validation of the audience's wholehearted applause.

As the night progressed, my confidence increased. I changed from the bathing suit into the formal dress; my newfound happiness and confidence exuded from every pore of my body. After I came off the runway and was putting on my regular clothes – ready to go home – my name was announced as the winner of both the Miss Fashionality and Miss South Philadelphia titles. It was a surprise beyond my wildest dreams. I had won not one, but two, contests that evening.

Ms. South Philadelphia Contest

Mrs. Lee's hard work in organizing the event paid dividends. The invited media showed up in droves to report on the outcome of the evening. When I was announced as the winner, all cameras turned in my direction as I was crowned – the flashlights popped, capturing the fleeting moment of pure joy. If only for those few minutes, I felt I was a winner for the first time in my life. I had been judged for just being me.

However, like Cinderella at midnight, my golden carriage turned into a pumpkin. The stark truth of my reality reappeared after I returned home; the taste of those euphoric few hours faded into the recesses of my mind. Yet, despite all my parents' efforts to continuously make me feel worthless, they could not take my prize away from me. While a small part of me wanted my adoptive parents to witness and acknowledge my achievement, I knew I would receive no accolades from them. Nor would they feel any sense of pride in their daughter. Perhaps it was their own feelings of inadequacy and lack of self-worth that led them to treat me so brutally.

All the local newspapers carried photos of the contest the next day, so it was impossible to keep it secret at home. Once my father discovered that I had won the contest, it produced a particularly harsh reaction from him. He felt threatened by my newfound self-worth. He lashed out with insulting taunts, calling me a slut and a whore – attempting to strip me of the validation I had received from strangers. He did manage to put an end to any notion I had of a career in modeling; I couldn't bear the thought of feeling permanently humiliated by him if I never succeeded.

Shortly after my win at the Miss Philadelphia contest, I received an invitation to take part in the Miss America pageant; but I knew by my father's reaction to the previous win that it would unleash brutal physical and emotional punishments. I tore the invitation to shreds and assigned it to the garbage can.

In the weeks and months after the beauty contest, I was baffled when my father unexpectedly began displaying affection and showing me some kindness. He would arrive home with chocolate cupcakes for me, bought at the bakery on his way home from work. It took me some time to realize that his scheming knew no bounds; my weight shot up from 125 to 160 pounds within the space of a year.

Once I finished high school, I wanted to cut ties with my parents and break out of the torture chamber that I called my home. Kathy and I often spoke about our home situations. She also had experienced a difficult home life with her father, and it didn't take much to convince her that there was a big world out there where we could experience real independence. With the naivete of youth, we hatched a plan to leave home and establish our autonomy.

Our first adventure was all of 300 miles away. Traveling by Greyhound bus, we headed south to the popular holiday spot of Virginia Beach. I had accumulated a reasonable amount of savings from all my odd jobs to keep us going. And within a matter of days after our arrival, we found jobs as waitresses in a diner off the main strip.

There was enough savings to last at least a month, and Kathy agreed that the most prudent option was to share a room in an inexpensive hotel. It was not the most salubrious hotel or in the safest area, but it suited our needs until we could afford to look for an apartment.

We were young, free, single, and full of hopeful anticipation. We thought that success would come and find us and it would be all so easy. However, that notion was quickly quashed by empty tables and idle hours at the diner, accompanied by a token wage and a reliance on meager tips. The reality was a lot harsher than our foolish dream.

On the first day of work, I was assigned to a group of tables, but no customers showed up over the entire eight hours of my shift. At the end of my work day, I handed my waitress uniform back and quit. We didn't have much hope that things would improve, so we had to rethink our strategy. The resort was a victim of the severe recession experienced across the US in the mid-1970s. Money was scarce, so people stayed home rather than chase to the beach on a holiday that they could not afford. The vision of a steady income faded into thin air for me as my savings dwindled. It took just a single day for me to appreciate that the restaurant or customer service type of environment did not interest me. The empty tables reinforced my gut instinct that there was something better on the horizon. I attributed the experience to the naivete of my youth and I matured a little that day; it was one of life's valuable lessons.

Kathy and I hung around Virginia Beach for a couple of more weeks before we decided to return to Philadelphia and familiar streets and faces. When I did finally get home, there was no warm welcome from my parents or any increased sense of security. My past experiences taught me to be wary around my father; his volatility remained as erratic as ever. I did my best to make myself invisible. I would disappear to my bedroom when he was home, or arrange to meet friends who lived nearby. I just stayed out of the house as much as possible to avoid having to deal with either my mother or father.

I started planning what type of career I wanted to pursue as I sized up my options. I considered working in an office environment, so I took a course in typing and shorthand to increase my chances of gainful employment. I was keen to take another bite at some level of independence. Considering that I managed to put myself through high school without help from my adoptive parents, I didn't expect any financial or emotional support from them after high school either. I always presumed that it was up to me to achieve the goals I had set for myself. I didn't want to live under their roof much longer; my aim was to get away from their abusive and controlling house. I lived in constant fear that the switch inside my father's head would suddenly flip and I would be an easy target when his explosive temper was triggered.

Kathy and I were back in Philadelphia only a couple of weeks when I received a notice from the United States government's Social Security Administration. I was invited to take an exam and interview for a vacant position with the agency. In those days, the US government had a recruitment policy to seek out students who had achieved high grades, but had not applied to go to college. The invitation was a result of the honors-level grades I achieved in my high school exams.

It was unexpected, and I was a little taken aback – but in a good way. I did not waste any time in confirming that I would be happy to sit for the exam. Then, after I passed the exam, I was contacted to interview for a civil service position. I immediately put on my interview clothes and high-heeled shoes, and took a bus to the Social Security Administration on Vine Street. Tucking my nerves into my purse, I switched on my best smile and gave it my all at the interview.

As luck would have it, I was hired as a secretary to the department head of the Reconsideration Determination unit. It was the beginning of the change that I craved – to begin to achieve self-sufficiency and stability. I was delighted and grateful for the opportunity to forge a promising new path toward a brighter future.

My new job provided me with an increased sense of self-confidence and security. However, I had never forgotten my family in Poland, and the idea of eventually reconnecting with them gave my life purpose. Many times, that thought was the only thing that kept me going. With an increasing sense of self-worth brought about by turning 18 (and becoming legally responsible for myself), I set about making contact with my biological family.

I felt mixed emotions – trepidation and excitement – when I started to write a letter to them. I would write and then tear up the paper, repeating that pattern for hours on end, until I was finally happy with the text.

I wanted to be satisfied that I had explained myself sufficiently. My home address in Poland had been chiseled into my brain before I even left Krasne as a child, so I knew where to send the letter. I decided to write the names of all three of my sisters, as well as my grandmother's, on the envelope.

One of my friends – who was sympathetic to my situation – made a generous and empathetic gesture. She encouraged me to use her home address for correspondence. That would ensure that my adoptive parents would remain ignorant of any efforts to reach out to my family in Poland.

Again, I addressed the envelope to the four most important women in my life – my grandmother, Helena, and my sisters Ela, Teresa, and Joanna. However, I was not sure if anyone would respond to the letter, or whether my family even still lived in the village. While I felt a little anxious about sending the letter, I was also curious to see what would come back. There had been a 10-year silence from my family and just one attempt on my part to reach them since I had left Krasne. Long-buried childhood memories were triggered. I wished with every ounce of my being that the ink on my letter would bridge the chasms of time and distance to reunite all of us.

Each day as the mail arrived, my heart skipped a beat in anticipation. As days turned into weeks, and then months, there was still no correspondence. Finally, many months after I had sent the letter, my friend called to say a blue airmail envelope had arrived in her mailbox – and it was from Poland! I headed to her house and picked up the letter before I went to work; I held it in my hands with much anticipation.

I rushed to the office and sought some privacy; I wanted to savor the long-awaited moment. I found an empty office where I could sit with my thoughts before delving into the envelope. My hands were shaking uncontrollably – I struggled to take out the letter with the longed-for words from home. The letter was in Polish. I grew frustrated trying to identify and translate familiar words. In the end I gave up, and waited to get home to rummage through some old books where I knew I had stored a Polish dictionary. As I painstakingly looked up each word, an uneasiness swept over me, and tears of disbelief and shock blurred my vision.

The letter was from my sister Teresa, but the words struck me as extremely odd – strange, even. There was no emotion, no compassion, and I found the narrative distressing with its cold and factual content. Its only real message was a request for money; the writing was only about the family's needs, and it contained no words of kindness, compassion or love.

I read and reread the letter, thinking that I must have missed something, but it was there in black and white. There was not a single inquiry about my welfare, or a mention of the years apart or family events I had missed. There was nothing specific about the family's current situation. Instead, the nonchalant manner of the text spoke of how difficult life had been for them and asked for some money to help out.

Several letters followed, always asking for one thing – for me to send money. I sent a few dollars on several occasions, but the niggling doubts that I felt when I received the first letter increased with each correspondence.

In one of my replies, I requested a photo, which was duly sent. However, as I searched the face of the woman pictured in the photograph, it sparked no memories. She called herself my sister, but she held no familiarity for me. I was thoroughly disappointed and disheartened. I decided that when I was a little older, I would go seek out my family in Poland for myself. Eventually, I stopped corresponding with this woman who claimed to be my sister.

Many years later, I discovered that my letters had been intercepted by the postman in Krasne, who knew my family. He was aware that I had been adopted and was living in America. That initial letter I had sent to Krasne had described my circumstances and the misery I endured since arriving in Philadelphia.

A chilling connection eventually emerged; I would discover that his daughter had shared not only my youngest sister Joanna's class, but also the same name as my older sister, Teresa – and the same family name. This charlatan of a postmaster decided that I was a cash machine that he could exploit. His actions were nothing but despicable; and he succeeded in delaying my family's reunion by many heartbreaking years. It was a duplicitous ploy, preying on my vulnerability to line his own pockets – and it left me with no option but to return to Poland someday and find my family.

* * *

My friendship with Kathy was always solid. We were constantly in each other's company, and she continued to make me laugh – always lifting my mood in the darkest of times. We had very different personalities, but our bonding came with our shared sense of being outsiders. In our friendship, we found solace from the world that seemed resolved to test us at every turn. We would sit and talk for hours on end about our lives and our ambitions. We had each other's back and understood each other's family situations. And we learned how to put all of our concerns aside once in a while and enjoy a little frivolity – as all teenagers feel that they're entitled to do.

Like most of our peers, we had fake IDs, and purses full of makeup that disguised our young years. Our IDs allowed us to frequent a neighborhood bar so that we could look for a bit of fun, belonging, and friendship. The local bar was a lively spot for underage clientele; and each Friday night it buzzed with that weekend vibe and lively music. It was on one of those Friday nights when we noticed a couple of handsome guys at the bar.

With the confidence of youth, we sidled up to the bar, and it did not take long before the two guys were chatting us up. Kathy was smitten with Jack from the moment she set eyes on him and she could talk of nothing else. They left the bar together; but I remained, chatting with Jack's friend, Mike. It was hard to ignore Mike's perfect physique and penetrating eyes. Not only was he handsome, but he also came across as a caring and kind person who listened to what I had to say. Mike made me forget my troubles; I felt reassured and protected from the chaos that life had hurled at me. When we parted, we agreed to meet the following week, and thus began a great friendship. Soon, that friendship would develop into something much deeper; I was 16 years old and in love for the first time in my life.

I was well aware that my family life would never be considered normal. Had I reported some of the abuse I received, I would have been removed from the family home by social services and fostered out, possibly to an equally dysfunctional family. I had walked a lonesome, loveless road, paved with violence. I had felt sadness and separation ever since losing my beloved mother, father, and sisters in Poland.

True, some of my friends may have had a tough time in their own homes, and may have even lacked some material things in life, but there was always one person in their family who could attend to their emotional needs. I was especially a little envious of my friends who had sisters. I had never stopped missing my sisters; and the separation was only compounded by my yearning for a real family to call my own. While I had a growing suspicion about the nature of the correspondence from Teresa in Poland, and her motivation, I was despondent about the chances of a reunion. So, I made a calculated decision to create my own family.

At that time, there were so many pregnant teenagers and teenage mothers across the US that it seemed almost as contagious as a flu virus. Our neighborhood was no different, and I too caught the "virus." In my case, I set out to do so intentionally. A simple pregnancy test confirmed what I suspected – I was to be a mother.

I dreaded the prospect of facing my parents with the news, terrified that it would set my father off on one of his violent frenzies. Their life revolved around church and the pretense that they were good Christians. A pregnant teen, *single* daughter usually signaled shame for a Catholic family. But for some unknown reason, my parents did not show any anger or annoyance when I announced my pregnancy, and I continued to live with that crazy family.

As with many other teens who found themselves in a similar situation, marriage was considered the best solution – regardless of the boyfriend's character or integrity. Marriage certainly would have been my parents' preference. Mike and I had been dating for three years when I became pregnant, but – as he had mentioned so often – he wasn't the marrying kind. I had no expectations of him changing his mind. I had a good job with the United States Social Security Administration, which included health insurance – and I felt more than capable of handling the situation. I did expect that Mike would provide support for our child, but again the cold hard reality of life would not match my expectations.

I was several months into the pregnancy when Beth, my friend from West Catholic High since my early teen years, called to tell me that she had seen Mike with another girl. Beth observed that Mike's actions around this mysterious girl did not indicate a platonic or sisterly relationship. Mike was cheating on me, and I felt betrayed. I had really expected some sort of loyalty to me and our unborn baby.

The mixture of hormones and anger were not a good combination, and I made a snap decision to end the relationship. I felt that I was doomed – here was yet another man in my life who was letting me down. It left me wondering why all the significant men in my short life turned out to be poor excuses for human beings. I started to believe that I couldn't attract a decent man as either a father or a partner.

I let it rip at Mike for "double-dating" me and showed him the door. I told him that I had enough problems in my life without voluntarily taking on another. He didn't put up a fight to keep me. In reality, I was gifting him freedom from responsibility. As he walked out the door, he muttered that he would be back when the baby was born in February.

But as the door closed behind him, I was left to contemplate my future. I was terrified when I thought about my prospects. While my head told me I had enough complications in my life and I had made a good decision, my heart was telling me a very different story. I was 19 years old, juggling a pregnancy and a totally dysfunctional family life. And to top it off, my heart was in smithereens, with little chance that it could ever be put back together again. I really didn't expect to set eyes on Mike again after he sauntered into the sunset and out of my life with his hands firmly placed in his pockets.

During that period, life at home was more peaceful, at a time when I needed that the most. I was employed; I was considered old enough to become a mother, and deemed to be an adult. My parents' acceptance of the pregnancy was a comfort.

I had foolishly convinced myself that we were turning into a normal family and that the seed of tolerance had borne fruit. However, my parents' hypocrisy in attending church each Sunday while committing evil behind closed doors turned me off. I no longer considered church a place where good people gathered, so I decided I no longer wanted to attend the weekly charade of appearing at Mass. I put my decision into action one sunny Sunday morning in August.

My mother and father noticed my no-show in church. Not long after the priest came onto the altar, my father stormed out of the church to go looking for me. Eventually, he spotted me several blocks away. He approached me in his Sunday suit, sweating profusely in the August heat, his face purple with rage. I was four months pregnant at the time and my little bump was beginning to show. Without a word, he walked up to me and punched me in the face so hard that I instantly hit the sidewalk in a heap.

As I looked up at him, he almost spat at me; and then, without saying a word, he turned on his heel and walked back to church to pray to his God. I lay on the sidewalk, struggling to sit up straight, which took me several minutes. I was a mess. I watched the blood pumping from my nose, soaking into my dress. It took me a moment to find enough strength to pull myself up. I was so weak that when I tried to walk, I found myself staggering like an old drunk.

Even in my dazed and confused state, one thing became patently clear – if I remained at home, he would end up killing me and my unborn baby. I had given Mike his marching orders and now it was time to finish with this so-called family. I needed to rid myself of the chaotic home and the crazy people.

After I made it back to the house, I collapsed on the porch, taking a rest while trying to gather my thoughts and contemplate my next move. The house had been my only home since I arrived in the US more than 10 years before. While I was beset with fear of the unknown, I knew I had just one option. Whatever fear I was experiencing, it did not overcome my resolve to get out of that house.

I could not think straight, let alone make a decision. Everything was up in the air. I sat on the porch for several hours as my parents remained praying in the church. I was trying to figure out my next step – a step that would change the trajectory of my life and allow me to take control of my future.

I knew my options were limited. After much thought, I called my friend Dee, who lived in the neighborhood. Her family was large and also Catholic, but at least there was a modicum of Christianity practiced in their home. Her parents lacked the hypocrisy I experienced with mine. There was no hesitation; Dee's family welcomed me with open arms, providing much-needed sanctuary, support, empathy and understanding. Although their home was already crowded, I was grateful for a couch to sleep on, with the added luxury of a breathing space to decide my next move.

My departure from home prompted my adoptive father to take revenge by keeping my car, most of my possessions, and all my precious photos and valuable documents. While his vindictiveness was expected, I knew it was not the end of the world. I was just thankful that one area of my life – my job – provided financial security through a steady source of income.

I adjusted to my unpredictable situation, living frugally and saving every penny for my baby's arrival. I started couch surfing, staying in the homes of different friends, and not overstaying my welcome so I would not become a burden. Kathy had moved on from Jack, and was in a relationship with a new partner. They had moved in together and I stayed with them in their one-bedroom apartment for more than a month, sleeping on the sofa. Unfortunately, their relationship was in its dying days, and they spent most of their time fighting, shouting at each other with tit-for-tat accusations. It reminded me of my experiences at home and why I had left.

My morning sickness was more like morning, noon and night sickness – it was relentless. I could barely hold anything down and was rapidly losing weight. Within a couple of weeks, rather than gaining pregnancy weight, I had shed 15 pounds, which took a heavy toll on me. I looked absolutely wretched and felt exhausted. Nevertheless, I had no choice but to show up for work each day, despite feeling so ill and weak. Kathy was happy to have me stay with her and made me feel welcome, but I hankered for a little peace and quiet and some privacy to deal with the persistent nausea. I started looking for a place to rent, and I came across a small apartment on the upmarket Snyder Avenue in South Philly. I rented the place on a temporary lease, but it did not take long before I realized that the rent was well beyond my means. It was eating into the savings I had set aside for the baby's birth. So, I was forced to reluctantly turn to my friends again to open their homes and provide the refuge I so badly needed.

My situation did not remotely reflect the life I had envisioned for myself. I had to address the challenges of the curve ball that had landed like an asteroid at my feet. Meanwhile, my nausea was so bad that on some mornings I felt as if I couldn't lift my head off the pillow. But I continued to show up for work – I had no other option.

My ankles failed me – they were swollen from the pregnancy and became weak – so I was continuously tripping over things, endangering myself and my baby. Despite being in my seventh month, I barely looked it, because of the debilitating morning sickness. By that time, I was staying with yet another friend who was generous enough to provide me shelter. The pressure of the baby on my bladder meant I was frequently rushing to the bathroom after every glass of water.

On one particular night, I was in such a hurry that I did not bother turning on the light. The family dog was lying in the middle of the floor. With my obstructed view and with the darkness, I didn't see the pooch, and I tripped and fell down. I hit the floor hard; within a matter of seconds, I began to bleed and started feeling contractions. Soon, I was in an ambulance, rushing to the hospital. I was alone in the hospital room – struggling to hold onto the pregnancy – and without one single family member or friend to provide comfort.

I kept thinking back to my own mother's pregnancies – the loss of Basia and my two brothers – and I prayed to my mother and grandma for a safe birth. I think I would have lost my reason if I had lost the baby – I had sacrificed everything for this. The doctor desperately tried to stop the birth; but after 24 hours of doing everything in his power – including his own prayers – he felt he had no option but to allow the baby to be born.

It was a difficult labor, and the doctor feared that neither I nor my baby would survive the process. But after several touch-and-go hours, my beautiful baby girl, Dana, arrived. She weighed in at just 4 ½ pounds, and I got to hold her briefly before she was whisked away and placed in an incubator. Because Dana's lungs had not developed sufficiently to allow her to breathe alone, she had to spend the first two weeks of her life in an incubator, in the care of the wonderful staff at the hospital. I visited her every day, dressed in a hospital gown and wearing a mask. I could put my hand into the incubator and her tiny hand would grasp my finger as I watched this amazing piece of humanity that I had brought into the world.

Before Dana could be discharged from the hospital, I went hunting for an apartment and found the perfect home for us. It was a busy few weeks, getting everything ready and making our "nest" as comfortable as possible. Time and time again, my memories took me back to my own childhood and my family's very humble beginnings. I thought about the sparseness of our existence, with zero luxuries to provide even a degree of comfort. I was reminded of the cold, the hardship, the poverty and the daily struggle we had experienced. I reflected on the loss of my mother and my grandmother's dedication to my well-being.

I made a vow that my daughter would not have to live with the kind of fear that I had experienced most of my life. I went shopping for furniture, and bought a Little Me brand crib for Dana. Simply looking down and seeing my daughter sleeping in her crib brought more than a few tears to my eyes. However, these were tears of happiness, mixed with a good dollop of immense joy.

Before Dana's birth, I had completed a six-month training course at work and was promoted to the position of exception examiner. It was a title that brought a lot more responsibility to my work, along with an increase in salary. It was an opportunity to start climbing a career ladder, elevate my position within the department, and provide the extra income that was required to support my baby. I felt fortunate and grateful to have found my job; my boss was not only cognizant of my situation, but also sympathetic. He authorized my application to take a one-year hiatus to look after Dana while the company would continue to pay 70 percent of my salary.

I loved being a mother, and I cherished the time spent with my daughter during the next nine months, despite the challenges that continued to land at my feet. I was facing the most important task of my life – to raise my daughter without a partner. I had not heard from Mike since he had walked out the door. Even as the expected due date approached, he was nowhere to be seen. For the first two months of Dana's life, I cared for her alone in our little apartment on Paschall Avenue. I was up every four hours to feed her; I wanted to make sure that, even as a premature baby who practically fit into one hand, she would have the best chance at life that I could provide. After several weeks, Dana fell into a regular sleeping pattern. I was able to start getting enough sleep and rest.

Then – a little late, but as he had promised – Mike reappeared in February. He had reached out to my friends to find me at my new apartment. I was not expecting any visitors when the doorbell rang, so I was surprised to see Mike standing there. He had heard the news from my friends and wanted to meet his daughter. I was not going to deny him access to Dana, so I invited him in.

He was thrilled to see the little bundle of pure happiness that we had created, and I welcomed a father's presence in her life. I watched his face as he picked his daughter up from the crib as naturally as the sun rises; and then I watched him instantly fall in love with her. He held her gently as she reached out her hand to grasp his finger, gurgling and smiling up at him.

I had to weigh my choices – I could decide to ask him to leave us alone and therefore deprive Dana of a father, or I could have him with us on our side. And so, I made the decision to allow him into our lives. Mike moved in and we resumed a relationship, as a family. However, in his short absence he had not exactly developed a sense of ambition. He preferred to babysit Dana while I went to work to support the family. There are no wiser words spoken than, "If you want to know me, come live with me." Mike exhibited no urgency to land a job or contribute to the household expenses, and he displayed a distinct disinterest in sharing any responsibility as a breadwinner.

We were complete opposites. I was anxious to create a secure and loving family home in which to raise Dana, whereas Mike was more concerned about whether there was beer in the fridge (rather than milk for Dana). I wanted to be able to provide my daughter with a good education and a normal family life. But Mike lacked the drive and motivation to secure steady work. Although I felt disheartened at times, there were still incredible moments of joy. Dana's giggles and smiles filled our home with love. While our path ahead was unclear, I knew that with a bit of hard work and optimism, we could find a way to create a better future. Life was a series of ups and downs, but I refused to lose hope. I chose to remain positive and focused on building a better life.

I watched Dana over that first year, fascinated at this growing baby. She wrapped me around her little finger as she cooed and smiled each time I came within a few feet of her cot or stroller. There were also times when I could not settle her, as it is with every baby. When she was teething, I spent many hours into the night walking up and down the floor with her in my arms, trying to calm her sobs and ease her discomfort.

I was ready to get back to work and had the energy for it when Dana was 9 months old. She had settled into a routine, so I did not wait for the one-year maternity leave to expire. Not only did I feel Dana was settled, but I also had a family to support – and trying to survive on 70 percent of my salary during my leave just wasn't sufficient. All in all, Dana was a very happy baby and demanded little else once she was fed, her diaper was changed, and she had enough sleep. She excelled in her role as a baby – cooing, laughing, and generally being a charming and lovable little bundle of wonder.

I could not help thinking of the joy my adoptive parents were missing by having no contact with their granddaughter. I wanted Dana to have it all in terms of a family life. I kept thinking about the human desire to be loved. And despite the beatings and mistreatments, I wanted to show my parents their first grandchild and make some effort at reconciliation.

I had not seen or heard from them in more than two years, and made a decision to take Dana to meet them; I wanted her to at least know her grandparents. By that time, Dana was already walking. I dressed her up in a pretty dress and we walked hand-in-hand up the pathway to my adoptive parents' house. As we did, memories hurtled into my mind like a storm wave crashing against the side of a cliff. I was nervous and my stomach was tied in a knot that refused to unravel. But I remained positive and hoped this visit would be a chance for reconciliation and understanding

We arrived at the familiar door and I rang the doorbell. After a minute or so, my adoptive father came to the door and stood on the other side of the closed screen. He was expressionless; with a blank stare, he looked us up and down, as if we were beggars calling for some charity or spare change. He never said a single word or unlocked the screen. He just stood there, looking at us blankly as if we were total strangers.

It was then that I realized that any attempt of reconciliation would be futile. Before we left home, I had told Dana that we were going to see grandpa and grandma. She was full of excitement, jumping around as I dressed her. However the cold reception we received was enough to send a shiver through the small child – Dana grabbed hold of my leg and looked up at me with confusion in those innocent eyes.

I mustered a smile and gently told her we had come to the wrong house. It was as if my adopted father had punched me in the stomach again. Such was his ability to project – even by his silence – the hatred he felt for me. We turned around and walked away; but I couldn't help feeling so hurt and disappointed as the tears welled up. I had been naive enough to think that they would want to rebuild our fractured bonds and welcome my beautiful daughter into their home.

I had gone to the house looking for understanding, with a willingness to forgive and move on. Instead, I was met with absolute rejection, and it hurt. I was finished with them; they had no meaning in my life and it was time to shift gears. I needed to consign the hatred and punishment they had dished out to me to the garbage can.

That was the last time I ever had contact with, or set eyes on, Adolph Czarnecki. His wife, Anna, never came to the door that day. When Adolph died around 2006, my cousin Michael let me know he had passed. Anna survived for a few more years before she, too, went to meet her maker. I did not attend either funeral.

I had no choice but to turn up my determination by several notches and harden my resolve. I now had the responsibility of a precious daughter, and I was not going to let anything or anyone get in the way of my plans. Mike's stay with us became a casualty of my newfound tenacity. I had enough to do between the responsibilities of my job and the baby without carrying the burden of a man with no ambition, who was a drain on my time and energy – and managed to create more work for me in the home. While Mike took great care of Dana – and I had no doubt he was great at taking care of her – I was looking for something else. I wanted an equal partner, someone as ambitious as I was, to work with me as a team to bring stability and security to our family.

Mike was happy enough in his role as Dana's minder. He had the benefits of free lodging, food on his plate, and beer in the fridge. However, he was not reading the room very well; he began dropping hints about marriage. I knew in my heart of hearts that it just would not work out as I weighed the pros and cons of marriage to Mike. We were opposites in personality, outlook, ambition, and attitudes. Any formal union would bring heartbreak for me, and misery for both of us, with an inevitable divorce. I also had to take into consideration how that upheaval would affect Dana in the future. I had no doubt that Mike absolutely adored his daughter and was a great father, but I was not so sure about his commitment to me. Marriage would only add to my everyday challenges, not solve them. And his change of heart came a little too late; I could still recall his nonchalant attitude when he walked out during my pregnancy, and the devastation I felt at that time.

Since Dana's birth and even before it, I had worked really hard to create a stable life for both me and my daughter, and I could not risk jeopardizing it for an unambitious man who did not share my vision. I was motivated to achieve greater financial security and wished for a partner who shared my dreams and aspirations. While I appreciated that he was Dana's father and that she adored her daddy, I made the painful decision to walk away and forge a new path alone.

I had a vision of a secure future that did not include Mike in my life. He left the following week; after finding an apartment nearby, he set up his new home, eventually living there with a girlfriend. In fairness to Mike, his new place was suitable for Dana to stay overnight in, with a separate bedroom furnished for her visits. I was never going to deny Dana the opportunity to bond with her precious dad.

I realized that I would be the only person to suffer if I continued to harbor any bitterness for the parents who had adopted me. Holding hate and anger in my heart meant they would remain with me permanently. The only thing I could do to save myself was to *let it go!* The pain and heartache stayed with me, but I held no feelings against them. Now, Mike and Dana were my little family – so I resolved not to nurture hatred. In doing so, a crushing weight was lifted from my shoulders, providing me with a lightness, a sense of optimism, and an impetus to move on. I realized that I could let go, transcend the bonds of my past, and embrace a future with limitless potential.

A series of extraordinary happenings…

Work was going well: I was respected in my job, and slowly but surely I was making my way up the career ladder. I had some excellent colleagues who in time became good solid friends, increasing and enriching my circle. In the absence of any family, my friends became my substitute family, providing the support and friendship I so craved.

I met Mary at work, where we were both in the same department. We were around the same age and we began to hang out, often meeting in the cafeteria for lunch. On some evenings, we would meet up and go to a concert or a movie. Mary was the most serene person I knew; nothing ever flustered or angered her. Whereas I was tall, she was petite, and she possessed a perfectly-proportioned svelte figure. Mary's slender figure had nothing to do with genes, but rather to her devotion to yoga and meditation; and so she introduced me to the wonders of this ancient art.

Even though I weighed nearly 15 pounds less than before my pregnancy, there were a few lumps and bumps that Dana unintentionally had gifted me, and I needed both toning and an increase in my fitness level. I began to practice yoga each morning, before Dana woke up or when she was napping, so I could begin my day with a focus on my own well-being. In no time at all, I was addicted to my morning routine – meditation and 20 minutes of yoga – finding serenity and an ability to focus on the tasks of the day. Any single mother will tell you that juggling motherhood with a full-time job can flip the stress switch. My new routine allowed me to look beyond the small irritations. It enabled me to step into a sunshine-filled day where I felt happier and more peaceful. While most of my friends were out doing what most people in their 20s were preconditioned to do – going to bars, concerts, camping and hiking, taking vacations – I was home with Dana, counting every cent that came through the door. All my earnings went to ensure that we would have a good home; and anything I bought for myself had to be on sale or a bargain. There was no room for trivial expenses.

I would buy books in bundles for $1, and every now and then I would come across a little gem that would spark my interest. One evening I stumbled upon *The Reincarnation of Peter Proud*, the story of a California university professor who had recurring nightmares and goes to the East Coast to try and find the location he saw in his dreams. It was a page-turning novel that generated a lifelong curiosity for me with its reference to the Bermuda Triangle and an unsolved mystery. I sought out and delved into books, fascinated with unusual phenomena and the stories that surrounded them.

In the evenings when Dana was put into her crib for the night, I would begin preparing for the following day. It was like a military drill; I would start with the cleanup after our dinner and then gather Dana's clothes and other belongings so that everything would be ready for when the babysitter would call to collect her in the morning.

I would often find myself standing by the bedroom window before I climbed into bed – peering through the shade and staring out into the night, lost in thought. It was a time to reflect on the day that had passed and contemplate the day ahead. I loved the peace I found when looking out over the neighborhood, imagining all the homes where friends and neighbors were preparing to put the day to rest.

One November evening, after the leaves had fallen and the clocks had fallen back, with the long winter evenings rapidly closing in, the tranquility of the moonless dark night was interrupted. As I stared into the sky, thinking over what had happened during that day and contemplating the next day's tasks, I did a double-take. Suspended in the air, across and above the row of homes, one house to the left of me, was an oval object, with panels of light in yellow, orange-red, and blue, slowly turning clockwise.

Mesmerized, I was unable to tear my gaze away from this astonishing phenomenon, this unidentified flying object (UFO). My heart was pounding and fear had an iron grip on my body, leaving me almost paralyzed. I felt panic rising through me. Even if I had wanted to scream, nothing was going to come out of my throat. I recall thinking that I would remember this strange event for the rest of my life. I noted that the UFO was the size of the rowhouse below and that it was only about 10 feet above the house. It made no sound as it hovered, almost as if it was suspended on an elastic band.

I realized that if I could see the object, there was something or someone inside it, also observing me. In my panic, I tried to get under the bed, but the bed was too low. My only other option was to dive under the covers to try to make myself invisible, terrified that it would all end badly. I stayed there for about 10 minutes or so, waiting for my heartbeat to slow to a more normal pace. When nothing happened, I finally gathered the courage to creep back into the living room and peep out the window again. The object was gone; it had disappeared, with no evidence that it had ever been there. What it did leave behind, though, was a lasting impact on my perception of the world.

When I arrived at the office the next day, I was eager to share my experience with my colleagues. Al was in charge of the department, a kind man who had always shown me respect. I excitedly shared the previous evening's strange encounter, hoping for understanding and validation. While he listened and smiled, others did not take my encounter seriously, dismissing it as a fanciful tale. But I know what I saw; and that extraordinary event forever changed my beliefs about the mysteries of our existence.

The next day, Al stopped by my desk as he was leaving work and told me he believed my story. There had been reports on the radio about an unknown object in the southwest Philadelphia skies the day before, near where I lived.

While some may doubt the extraordinary event that unfolded before me, I have come to believe that our world is filled with wonders beyond our comprehension. For me, the experience served as a reminder that life is far more intricate and intriguing than we can ever fathom. In the quiet moments, I still find myself gazing up at the night sky, wondering about the countless mysteries that await us. It's comforting that, amid the ordinary routines of life, there is always a chance for extraordinary events to occur.

* * *

It was the fall of 1977, and I was engrossed in my daily mundane reality. I was too busy to think of anything except getting through each day. I had accepted my lot and I was getting on with life. I channeled all the love from the core of my being into Dana; I had no inclination that my life was about to change in ways I had only dreamed of.

I received a phone call at home from a man who introduced himself as someone who was engaged to find me. (This was long before mobile phones, and there was always a possibility that a caller would not find someone at home to answer the phone.) The man on the line asked if I had a family in Poland and if I had been in a beauty pageant in Philadelphia. I was suspicious of the call, being from a total stranger, but he went on to explain that he was working for a Polish woman named Theresa, who lived in Chicago, and was a friend of my sister Ela in Poland. He had found me by searching through the telephone directory in Philadelphia, where my telephone number was listed. I went into high-alert mode, cautious after the fiasco with previous correspondence from Teresa in Krasne. Nevertheless, I was intrigued by the detail he was able to provide. I allowed him to continue the conversation.

After several minutes, I agreed to share my address to receive correspondence. Since my Polish-speaking skills were long since forgotten due to lack of use, I set down a condition that any communication to me needed to be in English.

I would find out that my grandmother and Ela had never forgotten me, not even for a day. Their family life was centered on a search to find me, like the missing piece of a jigsaw puzzle. Aunt Helena knew my adoptive father's people, the Czarnecki family. At one point, Adolph's niece came to visit Aunt Helena, and Ela went to meet with her. His niece told them that I was well and going to school, but that I missed my family in Poland. And whenever Grandma or my sister came across a person who was planning to travel to the United States, they would recount their distressing story of my adoption and our painful separation. They never once gave up hope for a reunion.

By the time Ela was in her late 20s, she was married with her own family and worked as a bookkeeper. She had a work colleague, Theresa, who happened to mention one day that she was planning to emigrate to the United States; it was arranged that she would marry a Polish emigrant and start a new life in Chicago. Ela set about befriending Theresa and shared the heartbreak of losing her little sister, with whom the family had no contact. Ela also described the tragedy of our mother's passing, my father's abandonment of his four girls, my grandmother's heroic efforts to try to keep the family connected, and the fateful separation that broke our family into pieces.

Ela worked her magic on Theresa, explaining with brutal honesty her heartbreak at losing me, and the never-ending quest to find her lost sister in the vast expanse of the United States. Theresa listened with empathy, and Ela entrusted her with the address of my adoptive family, where they believed I was living in Philadelphia. Ela begged Theresa to search for her sister in America and help in reuniting a family that was torn apart. While Ela was ever the optimist, the weeks turned into months, and then years, with no correspondence from Theresa in the US. She began to lose faith that there would be a breakthrough in finding me.

After a two-year silence that felt like an eternity, a tiny ray of hope surfaced. One of Ela's close friends had received a Christmas card from Theresa in Chicago mentioning Ela in the card, and the friend took it upon herself to pass on the sender's address. Ela was delighted with this piece of luck. She immediately sat down and wrote a letter to Theresa, where she expressed her disappointment at not having heard from her, and politely asked for the reason for the long silence. Ela also reminded Theresa of the promise she had made to find me in the United States. As it turned out, Theresa's silence was nothing vindictive, but more due to trying to settle into a new and very different life in the United States. As a newlywed with a young baby, it had taken some time for her to get established in Chicago; but she reassured Ela that she had not forgotten her or the promise to find her lost sister.

In Chicago, Theresa took it upon herself to enlist the services of a private detective, absorbing the fees and expenses. The detective was a guardian angel of sorts, who took on the challenge of pinpointing one Polish woman out of a population of over 200 million Americans. Before there was a Google search engine, or any general access to the internet, the detective began his search in Philadelphia, where he knew I went to live after my adoption. (According to Steinway Movers, the US is one of the most mobile nations in the world – the average American moves 11.7 times over a lifetime. So, it was somewhat unusual that I had remained in Philadelphia all those years.) I have so much to thank that detective for – he was unrelenting, never giving up in his search to find me.

After the investigator's call, I was impatient to move the reunion process along, although I was aware of the complexity of the situation. One evening in the fall of 1977, I arrived home from work with my arms full, juggling grocery bags and toddler paraphernalia. Dana was constantly chatting to me, recounting the minute happenings in her day at the nursery, and I was totally distracted while checking the mailbox before opening the hall door.

As I turned the key in the box, a solitary letter with a Polish stamp on it lay there. It was almost like it was speaking to me. I dropped everything to the ground, and I could feel the blood drain from my head – partly with excitement, and partly with a feeling of dread that the letter might contain bad news. My head was spinning, I shook uncontrollably – and like the breaking of a dam, the tears flowed when the longed-for words on the page became so blurred that I found it difficult to read.

The letter took the wind out of my sails; I was flabbergasted. My mind was racing with anticipation and excitement one minute, but in the next minute I was fearful that everything would be taken from me again. I was trying to focus on the positive; my sisters remembered me, and they too felt the pain of this cruel separation. The words in the letter instantly brought down the wall that I had built to protect myself from hurt and disappointment. All the emotion – all the memories of pain, beatings, and the loneliness and despair I had felt over the years, combined to hit me with a powerful force. I released oceans of tears for all those years where I felt abandoned and unloved.

Dear Krysia,

At last, we have found you. We've been dreaming about that for 13 years. We've been trying to get in touch with you. We wrote to your adopted father. We visited his sisters who live in Bialystok. His family told us a lot about you. We have learned from her that you want to get in touch with us too. That you still remember your Polish family. It was great – we are very happy about that. We believe we will regain you, although we thought you forgot about us first. We asked a friend of mine who was intending to go to Chicago to look for you, and she really started searching, which we are very grateful to her.

After so many years, I can write to you and expect an answer from you. I'm glad that you are on your own, so you will receive my letters easily. Your adopted father won't be against it. It's a pity you can't read and write

Polish, but I hope you will visit us soon and then we will talk and talk, and you will understand us and learn to speak Polish.

Darling, it isn't easy to write the first letter to you. After all, I am the oldest sister; my name is Elzbieta. I have lived and worked in Bialystok for five years. I have two children, a son, two years old, and a daughter, who is eight months.

Your second sister Teresa is still single. She works at a school near Warsaw. The youngest of us, Joanna (Asia), attends a grammar school. Last week the two sisters were at my place, talking about you. Even Joanna remembered many moments with you.

Krysia, you must know that we have always been thinking about you. It is going to be the happiest day when we will see each other. Let it be as soon as possible. We are looking forward to hearing anything from you. Tell us everything about yourself, what happened to you during all those years. We hope your letter will be long.

We send you a lot of greetings,

with love,

Elzbieta

With each passing day after I read the letter, I struggled to grapple with my reality. Who was I now? I felt as if I had a dual identity. I was a survivor of a turbulent childhood. I was a sister who had been lost in a foreign country for 13 years. I was an orphan. I was a granddaughter. I was an adopted daughter. I was a mother. I was a sister. I was an American. I was Polish. The weight of my multiple identities bore down on me, and I searched the mirror for some clue to my identity. I could not stop crying as I attempted to reconcile my past with the present. I felt like I was spiraling into an abyss, disassociating from the life I had built in America – yearning to find my true self.

Through the tears, I would find relief in the written words I exchanged with my sister. In each subsequent letter, I tried to help her understand the solitude I had experienced and that gnawing gap – that yearning for something I could not name, but that was part of me for so many years. I was transported back to my childhood; I looked upon Ela as my surrogate mother, her empathy and understanding transcended language barriers. Each time I sat down to write to her, the box of tissues was my companion to wipe away the tears. Armed with a Polish dictionary, I poured my heart into each response, seeking closure and healing. It was a cathartic process, and I was very grateful for the opportunity to unburden myself from the trauma brought by separation from my family and the unbridled hate unloaded on me by my adoptive parents.

As I navigated the emotional turmoil, I noticed that Dana was confused – she seemed to have absorbed the effects of my turmoil. Who could blame her? She was trying to comprehend what was happening to her mom as I sat there crying my heart out every evening.

I knew I had to keep myself together and stay strong for her. I did my best to simplify things and explain what it meant to me to be reunited with my family. It was a delicate balance between facing my past and embracing my present, all while providing comfort and love to my precious little girl.

The bond among my sisters and I grew more robust with each letter exchanged. It is so easy to forget that in the 1970s, the cost to make phone calls abroad was prohibitive; you almost had to take out a bank loan to do that. I began to feel more relaxed about the correspondence and looked forward to each letter that came into the mailbox.

In the first letter I received from my sister Teresa, she requested that I write and send her a letter of invitation to the United States. While I thought the request was a little unusual, I obliged, not questioning her motivation.

The process began, and after some time she was granted a visa to visit the United States. I dipped into my savings to cover the cost of the flight. I was sacrificing hard-earned money that I had put aside for a rainy day, but the anticipation of seeing one of my sisters in person on US soil trumped any thought of future expenses.

I eagerly awaited Teresa's visit with a mixture of exhilaration and nervousness. I was finding it difficult to sleep or concentrate. I was imagining our reunion and the conversations we would have, playing them over and over in my head. I wanted to find out about everything that had transpired in my absence, all the things that had happened – things that could not be described in a letter. After 13 years lost, 13 years of silence, the door of reconciliation was finally opening. My reunion with Teresa held the promise of healing and recovery. I wanted to believe that the past was done and that I could look forward to a bright future, closing the gap between my two very different worlds.

I prepared for Teresa's arrival, clearing out space in the one-bedroom apartment for her. Dana was also full of excitement, in expectation of meeting her aunt for the first time. As the day of Teresa's arrival came, I had everything gleaming and scrubbed. The bell rang, and I opened my door to greet my long-lost sister. I had imagined the scene – a joyous reunion of laughter and tears – but when I reached out to Teresa with an embrace, I found her somewhat indifferent and unresponsive. I was visibly shocked – and I'm sure it was written all over my face just how taken aback I felt. It was a non-verbal punch in the gut, which left me feeling absolutely bewildered.

Our relationship as children in Poland was often awkward, and it was evident that the years of separation had not brought us closer. If anything, the separation had pushed us farther apart. The memories of childhood disagreements returned, clouding the promise of a newfound bond. I hankered for the connection that had eluded me for so long, but instead I faced this unrecognizable version of a cold, elusive Teresa.

When she arrived, she spoke no English, and so our communication was difficult. However, I persisted in trying to communicate with my limited Polish. But despite all my effort to try to connect with this woman who shared my DNA, she showed very little interest in sharing stories of our lives. She focused more on her own needs and wants, which was disappointing.

Teresa had just one interest, and that was Teresa. She demanded money for clothes and makeup, saying that her appearance affected her self-worth. There was no recognition or gratitude for the sacrifices I had made – living on a few dollars a day so I could save enough money for her flight to the United States. It was really disheartening to see that she was so self-absorbed, with her priorities centered solely around her own needs.

Indeed, Teresa's presence in our lives caused discord; rather than embracing my daughter as part of my family, she pushed Dana away and demanded to be the center of attention. Her distant demeanor was off-putting; but I chose to try and understand the difficulty she experienced in growing up behind the Iron Curtain, in a country that offered little opportunity. I decided that empathy was the most productive path. I tried my best to make life easier for her. However, that became more difficult with time, and I began to question whether it was worth the effort to reconnect with my Polish roots and family. I desperately wanted that connection; but I could not bear to think that my other siblings would have attitudes and demands similar to Teresa's.

I pushed those thoughts to the back of my mind; rather than dwelling on the past, I focused on the love and strength I provided for my daughter. I found solace in knowing that I was giving Dana the best life I could afford. Ultimately, I realized that the love and closeness that I sought might not come from my Polish family, but rather from the bonds of friendship I had built in America. I realized that these were the people who truly cared for me.

Teresa was single and did not feel any compulsion to return to Poland – to her job or the family. In Poland, she had worked as a teacher in a small school without much prospect for the future. She settled into life in the US, overstaying her visa, and continued to live with Dana and me in our tiny apartment. Teresa spoke little English when she arrived, and perhaps that contributed to our contentious relationship as I grappled to relearn my long-forgotten mother tongue. Recalling my own difficulty to make myself understood when I arrived in the States, I paid a Polish nun a small amount to teach Teresa the basics of English – greetings, directions, etc. I wanted Teresa to know enough English so that she could make her way around without going into panic mode and getting lost. Kathy from the office had a friend who was of Polish descent, and she knew that Teresa was totally reliant on me for any social life, so Kathy introduced Teresa to this friend.

After an introduction, they began dating, and I was happy to see Teresa start to have a life of her own. Gradually, her dependency on me decreased, and that lightened my burden and responsibility. Teresa was married within six months of meeting this man. It was a small ceremony in a registry office, with few family or friends attending, but it was what she wanted.

Before the ink was dry on the wedding vows, Teresa was attending classes for immigrants, which allowed her to apply for citizenship and shift her focus to becoming fluent in English. She was also able to apply for a green card, which meant she could seek work and hold a job. It was a relief when she moved out of our cramped apartment and in with her husband, leaving Dana and me to enjoy our space and resume a safe and regular routine.

The experience with Teresa left me with a sense of uncertainty and a real fear of reconnecting with the rest of my family in Poland; but I needed to find out for myself. Certainly, the letters from Ela came across as warm and loving, and I continued to consider her my surrogate mom. I was as attached to Ela as I was to my grandmother. After giving it some consideration, I made a decision to go and see with my own eyes what connecting with my family would be like. I made plans for traveling; it was the only way I could finally move on with my life.

I was still haunted with the childhood trauma meted out by my adoptive parents when I began to plan my journey to Poland in 1978. But I realized that they had kept all the necessary documents I required for travel. Nevertheless, I was determined not to return to their house and provide that evil couple with the opportunity to further reject and humiliate me. I had zero regrets about leaving the toxic relationship with them.

I needed to reapply for the documents, but it was far from simple. It became even more complicated by the fact that I had no other familial bonds in the US to lean on. My first challenge was to retrieve the adoption records and certificate of naturalization from the Philadelphia courthouse. This was in the days when computers were more primitive and reliant on dial-up internet connections, and information was not as readily available. There was still no such thing as Google or other online search engines, so data was difficult to retrieve. The physical task of searching through dusty records was painstaking, involving many hours in the courthouse archives to locate the necessary documents.

I was piecing together the fragments of my past – trying to gather the necessary proof of my existence, and to establish a legal entitlement to live in the United States. After a number of weeks, I finally tracked down what I needed, and with the crucial documents in hand I was able to begin the process of applying for a Polish visa. There was enough in my savings account to afford the flight to Poland, but I had to use all my vacation leave from work.

This was my opportunity to rediscover and reunite with the family I had left behind so many years ago. I had to see for myself if circumstances and the daily grind of living behind the Iron Curtain had brought out traits similar to Teresa's among the rest of my estranged family members.

As a communist country, Poland had a reputation for notorious levels of bureaucracy, and the reputation was not exaggerated. Navigating the complexities of obtaining a visa to a communist country was no easy task, and I was baffled as to how to begin. I consulted with Teresa, who was familiar with the process, and she gave me a name and provided an introduction to a Polish diplomat who was attending the United Nations General Assembly in New York. I reached out to the diplomat, and he agreed to meet with me; but because he was so busy with meetings and appointments, our meeting had to take place in New York.

Other than the adventure to Virginia Beach with Kathy a few years earlier, I had not stepped outside Philadelphia. I was as excited as when I was a child on my first trip outside Krasne to the dentist that day with my mother. This time, I was grateful there was no tooth to be extracted, but I felt like a child again with the prospect of seeing and experiencing New York City. As I embarked on the train to New York, I had no way of knowing that the trip was to be the first of my many adventures there.

It was September 1978, and I arrived at Grand Central Station, one of the most elegant and spectacular buildings in the city. The energy of Manhattan was palpable as well as contagious. It seemed to ooze from the people as well as the buildings – I found myself in one of the greatest cities in the world. My head was constantly turning as I looked up to identify some of the most iconic buildings. I was mesmerized by the sheer size of the skyscrapers. I was trying to absorb the sights that were so familiar to me from movies and TV shows as I made my way to the United Nations headquarters on First Avenue.

Despite all the chaos in today's world, the United Nations still symbolizes hope, promoting peace and international cooperation. The sheer size of the United Nations campus could be compared to any small town in America. The first time I arrived at the United Nations building, the General Assembly was in process – a gathering of diplomats from around the world to address and resolve important global issues. As I walked in through the entrance, I was struck with the sheer height of the ceilings and the stunning symbolic artwork in the reception area, which added to the grandeur. I felt intimidated, and in awe of the symbolism it represented.

At the security post, I showed my identification, had a photo taken and was issued a permit to enter. An escort brought me to the lobby, where I met Teresa's diplomatic contact. I was so nervous – every part of me was trembling, and when he reached out to shake my hand, it would have been impossible for him not to notice. I greeted him in my limited Polish, which brought a wide grin to his face. Once the greetings were dispensed with, we reverted to English and took the elevator up to an office that was booked for the meeting.

I knew that this man was my *Willy Wonka* – he held the golden ticket that would unlock my past and reunite me with my family in Poland. He listened intently to my story. He seemed empathetic as I explained just how much I needed to see my sisters. I told him about the 13 years lost, and how my siblings had miraculously found me, which led to our intense correspondence. I told him of my need to reconnect the pieces of my past and that I felt that peace of mind was now within my grasp. As a family man, he recognized the significance of family and understood how much it meant to me to return to the place of my birth. This lovely gentleman guided me through every step of the visa application, supporting me through the bureaucracy – so much so that I started to believe in miracles.

During the visit to the United Nations, as I looked around, I could observe the diversity of the people from every country in the world who came through its doors – these were all employees. They worked in areas that aspired to bring justice, equality, and human rights to marginalized societies throughout the globe – laudable aspirations indeed, I thought. I casually mentioned that the United Nations must be a wonderful place to work. In reply, my newfound friend suggested that I drop into the United Nations personnel office while I was in the building and pick up an application.

Most of the professional positions within the United Nations required a master's degree or higher, so my hope of securing employment there had to be through the secretarial route. I was lucky that I had my qualifications with honors from high school, but I was apprehensive that I would not get beyond the initial application. I decided to throw in my hat anyway. At the time I visited New York I had already completed five years with the Social Security Administration, and I was ready for a change. The Polish diplomat encouraged me to explore the possibilities there, and he talked me through what would be required before I would be invited to take the entrance exam. The thought of working for an organization that was making a difference in the world excited me, but before I could even contemplate that idea, I needed to focus on the most important thing: traveling to see my family in Poland.

After completing a plethora of administration procedures with the State Department, I found myself in possession of my first US passport, a valid visa to communist Poland, and an airline ticket in my hand. By that time, it had been 14 years since I had left the only life I had known as a child to live in America.

I was so discombobulated about the trip that I felt I couldn't possibly cope with the responsibility of having Dana accompany me. I made a decision that it would be best if she did not come along. But I had to consider my options: Mike was working, and not in a position to take Dana for a few weeks; and I was worried that Teresa wouldn't be a suitable guardian – despite living with us for so long, she never bonded with my daughter.

I maintained the friendship with Terry and Beth when we left high school and we kept in frequent contact. When Terry heard of my upcoming trip she kindly stepped in and offered to take care of Dana. So I trusted my instinct, and left my darling daughter in the capable care of Terry – knowing that she would prioritize Dana's well-being and safety in my absence.

My return to Poland was very much a journey to find myself. It was a journey I needed to complete alone, without distractions. I had such conflicting emotions about my Polish identity and my life in Philadelphia – they were like parallel universes. Once I received the initial letter from Ela in English, all of her further correspondence came in Polish, which required several hours and a dictionary to painstakingly decipher the contents. But after a few months, words in Polish would pop into my head – and I was amazed at how I was beginning to translate English into Polish without thinking.

Reigniting my mother tongue could only be compared to taking an old rusty engine and pumping it with oil to provide it with a new lease on life. I began to dream in Polish again, a sure sign that my brain was receptive to reconnect with my family. I did not realize the importance of relearning my native language until much later, and how speaking Polish provided that core connection to my family and the home of my birth. Becoming more proficient in the language also provided a greater understanding of my mother and grandmother's culture and what made them such strong women.

Preparing for the trip was nerve-wracking, and part of me was dreading the journey ahead. I was going back to the bosom of my family. Yet, I recognized that some of the trauma I had experienced as a child remained and was combined deeply with the suffering and distress I went through with my adoptive parents. I was walking a tightrope of fear, but desperately trying to suppress that fear. At the same time, I knew I would be coming face-to-face with a part of my past that could push me over the edge in terms of my mental health.

My fear came from knowing that I could possibly face a similar rejection again. Was I capable of reconciling these parallel universes I had lived in for so long? What if I ended up in a mental institution? I prayed to God that if I lost my mind, I would just die, because I could not possibly continue to live through such hell. Death would be preferable. I also meditated; I asked for strength and the clarity to see me through a voyage that would bring me closer to the answers I sought, and for the closure that had eluded me for so long.

As the day of my flight approached, I had to devise ways to protect myself and my mental health. I envisioned a parallel universe where I could process events and activities without judging others or allowing others who made judgment about my life to affect me. In that universe, I could allow myself to think, feel, and cry – with either joy or disappointment – in preparation for what lay ahead. It was a momentous event in my life; I realized that unquestioning family support had been missing from my life for the longest time.

It was June of 1978. The trip back to Poland was as much a leap into the unknown as the first time I landed in America. I was so terrified of what the journey would bring that I have no memory of any of the details of the flight. What I do remember was the shock I felt when we landed in Warsaw; there were armed soldiers on the tarmac, pointing rifles at us as we disembarked.

It struck me that I was entering another world, going behind the Iron Curtain where my family was trapped with few freedoms or opportunities to control their own lives. Communism was dictated by an autocratic hierarchy similar to how the Catholic church was dominated by priests. Both institutions claimed to have the public's interest at the heart of their rhetoric, and both were heaving with hypocrites.

On arrival, I picked up my luggage and came through customs and immigration. I desperately scanned the crowds for a familiar face. I finally recognized Elzbieta from the photos we had shared; and I saw other family members who were laden with bunches of flowers, eagerly waiting for my arrival. It was as magical and as thrilling a moment as I have ever experienced – one that I had never thought would come to fruition.

I walked toward the small group where Ela stood. This gathering consisted of *my people, my kin*, all of whom had come out to greet their long-lost family member. I was wrapped in love, swathed in a circle of joy, each person crying like a baby with the sheer relief of finally having me back in the home of my birth.

It was a strange experience – I was reconnected to a part of my history that had been buried deep within me for years; yet, I stood there a stranger in my own land. The woman I had become was unrecognizable compared to the girl who had left so many years before.

We made our way back to the apartment in Warsaw where I had spent the last evening before I left Poland all those years ago. It was home to some cousins who hosted uncle Marion and me before I left for the airport. I was surprised at how familiar it was to me – I had only stayed there a couple of nights before my departure in 1964.

We sat around an oblong table in the apartment; I looked into the eyes of 12 people with whom I shared DNA. They were a mix of uncles, aunts, cousins, and nephews – in addition to my own beautiful sister. The mood turned from one of joy to sadness, and then from tears to laughter. We reflected on all those missed events and moments that should have been shared; but then we returned to the simple joy of my family embracing me into their loving sanctuary. It was surreal – it was as if I stepped into a dream, and I kept pinching myself to confirm my new reality. A combination of years of searching, a galaxy of hoping, and a universe of luck combined to make me the most grateful person on the planet.

The next day, we drove to Ela's apartment, where I stayed for much of the time on this first visit. Her husband, Henrik, my brother-in-law, was a perfect host; I was welcomed with open arms, and the whole family went out of their way to ensure my comfort. They provided space for myself and Ela to catch up; we had so much to talk about. I frequently had to ask Ela to slow down; while my Polish had improved considerably, I sometimes required a lot of concentration to process the language. It was so good to connect with Ela's children – my niece and nephew, Adam and Ewa (Eva).

I had thought about Elzbieta often over the years and had closely held the memories of this surrogate mother who emanated love and kindness. The reality of seeing Ela again lived up to my memories; after all of those years, she was still the embodiment of love. She filled the emotional abyss left by my adoptive mother and stepped straight back into her role as surrogate mom, showering me with tenderness and care.

Ela became my tour guide and champion as we navigated the series of meetings with our relatives. She relished showing me off; I felt like the winning ticket in her lottery. Each renewed encounter with another family member was a cause for celebration. Again, there were plenty of tears and laughter, where tables overflowed with traditional Polish food and gallons of vodka. There were no visible signs of wealth among my kin, but if hospitality was gold, they could have filled Fort Knox 10 times over. I savored every moment of reconnecting with my roots.

While there was much joy and excitement in my homecoming, there were other, more sobering, occasions that left me reeling with anguish. One of those occasions was a visit to my grandmother's grave in Krasnopol. Grandma had been buried next to my mother in the graveyard beside the church where we had gone to Mass each Sunday.

A deeply religious woman, my grandmother had always spoken about her fervent wish to die on Good Friday, as Jesus had. She fulfilled that prophecy when she passed on Good Friday, March 27, 1970. At the time of Grandma's death, my sister Joanna was living with her in the cottage. In the late 1960s, Uncle Henryk and his wife Wanda had decided that Joanna needed to go back to Krasne and live with her grandmother. Maybe it was because Grandma was getting on in years, and because it would have been good for her to have company after I left. Joanna would have been around 11 years old at the time, and slept with Grandma in the same bed.

That Good Friday in 1970, when Joanna woke up, she realized that Grandma wasn't breathing, and tried gently shaking her to get a response. When Joanna could not rouse Grandma, she realized she had passed away during the night.

It was a devastating blow to lose the enduring matriarch who was the center of the family. According to Ela, Grandma never gave up hope that I would return to Krasne someday. Her prayers were answered, albeit too late for me to feel her arms around me, or to see her smile, or to even bid her farewell. I placed flowers on her grave and prayed that she was reunited with my mother, silently thanking her for the gift of love and compassion she so generously provided to our little family.

As the days unfolded, I immersed myself in my Polish family's stories, traditions, and culture. The smell and the unique taste of food brought back memories of those early days when my mom and grandma would stand together at the stove, cooking silently in pure harmony. I remember it being so seamless for them, almost like a choreographed cooking session, as each dish was laced with dollops of love.

The language of my birth that had faded into the recesses of my mind was resuscitated as my memory muscle reactivated. Relearning Polish allowed a deeper bonding and connection to my family. I began to feel that sense of belonging that had been missing for so long in my life. Not only was I welcomed back, but my family let me know that I was missed and wanted. The journey to Poland was more than just a physical return – it was an emotional reunion. I felt deeply grateful. All those times that I had been lost in solitude and drowning in hopelessness were put aside; my dream had come true and I treasured every moment.

In the years before Grandma's death, there was no reconciliation between her and my birth father. Once Grandma passed, my father proceeded to dismantle her four-room house – the home he once shared with my mother and his children – brick by brick. He rebuilt it in Krasnopol and took Joanna there to live with him and his new family.

Ela organized a visit to this man who had barely made an appearance in my life, and of whom I had little memory. It felt weird, at best. It was another totally surreal situation – to be back in the home where I had spent the first nine years of my life, but in a different location. I was meeting this stranger I barely knew, but who was part of my past. This man never displayed much affection or love; yet without him, I would not exist. There was no emotional reunion between us, but a polite acknowledgement of his significance – or lack thereof – in my life. He had two daughters with his second wife, Helena – Danusia and Mariola.

My two half-sisters were teenagers when I met them. I was unexpectedly swayed by their energy, which was mixed with a generous spirit and kindness. They welcomed me with warm embraces, and without hesitation they melted any doubts that may have lingered in my mind about them. We formed a bond when we met, and they became part of my family and my future.

Joanna was not informed of the time of my arrival at the house, but when she returned later that evening, she greeted me shyly, looking out under her eyelashes. We shook hands like strangers, but within seconds, the three sisters were embracing in one enormous bear hug. That night, for the first time in many, many moons, we slept in the same house – the house that was once home to all of us. It was where we lived in a bubble of isolation, ignorant of the outside world; yet, we had been gifted with happiness, security and love. As I drifted off to sleep, I conjured up an image of my mother and grandmother, and silently prayed that they were looking over us. I pictured them smiling and finally at peace to see this long-lost daughter returned to the fold.

The following morning, I woke before the sun came up. Not wanting to disturb the sleeping house, I dressed quickly. Then, quietly, I slipped out the door to explore the village of my earliest memories; I began the trek towards Krasne. I wanted to test myself to see if my memory was true, or constructed to fit a narrative in my mind to compensate for years of isolation and hurt.

An autumn mist shrouded the landscape as the sun began to rise. As I walked, the pall of the mist lifted to reveal the vast expanse of fields. I felt a deep sense of nostalgia. While I made my way towards Kranse on that beautiful morning, I felt my grandmother's presence at my side, guiding me past the fields. Many of the fields were already harvested with wheat stacked high, while others waited for the crops to be gathered. This area was the breadbasket of Poland, which would provide sustenance in the oncoming winter months for people in the farming communities who worked the land. Surplus wheat would be sent on to the city markets across the country.

I felt a certain sense of relief that my memory was not deceiving me. The familiar landmarks along the roads brought fresh memories of the long-forgotten treks to church. I could have been traveling in a time machine; I mentally hit the rewind button. In my mind's eye, I saw a more innocent, younger self, skipping alongside Grandma, dressed in our best Sunday clothes as we made our way to give thanks for our blessings.

Arriving at a crossroads, I relied on my instinct and chose the road to the right. I was in no hurry as I ambled along the worn pathway, enjoying each step and savoring every moment. I allowed the scents of the countryside to shake my memory and I savored the gentle breeze. It felt like minutes, but somehow hours had passed. As I approached a hamlet, I nervously asked a lady on the path if I was in the village of Krasne. Her smile confirmed that I had arrived back home.

As a young child, I would visit the neighbors in the village on most days, sometimes sent by Grandma with her cures and potions. On other days, I would call in to see if the older neighbors needed me to do anything for them. My dearest childhood friend and neighbor, Jagoda, still lived in the village. Although a few years older, Jagoda had been happy to have me as a friend.

When I arrived, I sought her out at her home. I wandered the familiar street, searching for her house until I finally found it. Although it was about 6:30 in the morning, I knew that the household would already be up and about. With a deep breath, I gathered my courage and knocked on the door. As the door opened, revealing Jagoda's mother, the years of my absence were blown away like a blast of wind across the lake. She took one look at me, and without hesitation or need for confirmation, she was shouting

"Krysia, Krysia, Krysia!" She threw her arms around me, laughing and crying at the same time. Her infectious ebullience touched my essence and I was embraced like a long-lost daughter.

Jagoda and her mom had heard that I was visiting the area and they were expecting a knock on the door. There was no question about it – I had to stay for food and sit at the table with the family. The ingredients for homemade Polish *kielbasa* were produced, a classic symbol of the hospitality they wanted to share. I sat listening to the two generations working together to prepare the food while the scent of cooking permeated the kitchen. I was at perfect peace.

The food preparation merged with the melody of conversation in a house where I had spent so many happy hours as a child. A sense of wonder overcame me as I sat there, taking in the sights and sounds of my forgotten homeland. In the background, the radio played a familiar American song, reminding me that I was straddling two merging yet disparate worlds.

Later in the day, I visited the plot next door where my former home once stood. The outline of the house site was still visible; and as I walked the ground I could spot the strawberry patch with some overripe fruit, indicating that strawberry season was good that year. The withered flowers in the garden were a reminder of past summer days when the house was filled with their scent; but now they seemed to represent the emptiness of those years lost to me. Nature has a funny way of reminding us of the circle of life; no matter what happens, the world still travels around the sun, and nature left to its own devices will persevere long after we have left this earth.

I had stepped through a tunnel, immersed in a past life. I had also lost track of time, and suddenly realized it was late and the sun was setting. I said my goodbyes to Jagoda and her mom, promising to return on my next trip. As I prepared myself for the walk back to Krasnopol, my father miraculously appeared on his tractor, knowing exactly where he would find me. We traveled back together along the bumpy road in silence. I felt no bitterness or anger; I was lost in thought, contemplating the events of the day in my mind, frequently smiling, relishing the joy of this special reunion with my friend and her family. I felt pure gratitude. The following morning, Ela and I bade farewell to my birth father's family and we continued on our journey.

During the trip, I allowed myself to live in the moment and cherish the gift of family and friends. For me, it was several weeks of pure indulgence – where I was welcomed, accepted without judgment, and bathed in pure love. The blissful homecoming marked a significant turning point in my life, leading to a journey of self-discovery and eventual recovery. My journey to Poland was a pilgrimage, a path of healing. I was reconciling my past and present with the promise of better days ahead.

However, the reality of life on my return to the United States soon left me deflated. The rollercoaster ride and adrenaline rush of meeting my family faded quickly, and I was left trying to reconcile my two identities. I was 23 years old and drowning in depression, grappling to find a way out.

The food in Poland was so good that I gained 10 pounds in the few weeks I was there, and I continued eating on my return. The weight continued to pile on. The weight gain was partly as a result of the inner turmoil that thrust me into a state of disconnect from everything and everyone. I considered that it was possible that the visit to Poland had reignited all the emotions that I had buried so deeply in an effort to protect myself. Moreover, I felt no one could understand the trauma I had lived through. I felt like an anonymous voyeur, observing my own life from a distance.

Even though I had reconnected with my family and was reassured by their love and affection – and likewise received validation from my loyal friends – I just could not shake off a sense of isolation and loneliness. There was so much wrong with what I had experienced as a young child. And I could not see the obvious: I had overcome situations that many grownups would have succumbed to. I was a born survivor – not only a survivor, but one with steel determination.

What I could not reconcile was the dueling identities – the two lives I had lived to that point. I felt despair at the squandered emotion and time: the absolutely unnecessary and depraved cruelty of my adopted parents. They were solely responsible for the pain of my separation from my blood sisters and adoring grandmother. The irony of it all was that had they given me even a modicum of love, they would have received dedication and loyalty. I would have jumped through hoops for them and returned that love in spades.

To have missed seeing my grandmother one last time played on my mind – another wasted, pointless outcome. I struggled; I would get up each morning, sit at the table with a box of tissues, and weep uncontrollably before I left for work. I could not find a way out of the misery – the tears were a release from everything that was bottled up inside me. I had to keep my focus on prioritizing my daughter, which thankfully kept me on the straight and narrow. She was the beacon of light in my life; but try as I might, I could not completely shield her from the impact of my emotional struggles.

It was in the middle of all my internal chaos that I received an unexpected call from the United Nations. They confirmed that my application was successful, and that I had passed all the entrance exams and the interview. There was a position open – and I was selected to fill the vacancy! The chance to work at the United Nations came at a time when I was probably at my lowest point; I saw it as the lifeline I needed, something to shift my focus and an opportunity to find purpose and direction.

I gave a month's notice to quit at work. Perhaps because of my state of mind upon returning from Poland, I found it emotional to be leaving the people who I relied on at work. They had become a kind of family. I was so grateful for the opportunities afforded me by that great bunch of colleagues, and my departure was met with tears and farewells. I packed up my apartment and prepared for a new chapter in my life.

New York

The route to employment with the United Nations is paved with onerous onboarding procedures, involving all sorts of paperwork, including references and health checks. But when everything was in order and all procedures were checked, I moved my life to New York City. It was June 1979; Dana was temporarily staying with Terry, who was by then married with a few children of her own. She was someone I trusted implicitly with the welfare of my daughter.

I needed to find a place to live, and opted to stay in the YWCA while I started work and began the search for a home for myself and Dana. I would leave work every evening, armed with the New York Post's rental properties section as I set off to view suitable accommodations for our little family. I decided to live in Queens, just across the bridge on the East River and just a few stops from Manhattan on the subway. I opted to share a house with an older, mature woman, who provided an easy sense of security, and where I was comfortable knowing that Dana would have a caring presence during my work absences. The place was close enough to my job, but a comfortable enough distance from Manhattan to provide a real community and neighborhood. Dana was enrolled in a new school, close to our house, as she entered first grade.

While my daughter was an adorable bundle of joy in my life, I struggled to balance the demands of motherhood, the responsibilities of my job, and the overwhelming emotional unrest within me. Deep down, I felt swamped. The pressure of being a single mother in a bustling city, the stress of coping with a new job at the United Nations with all its unfamiliarity, and my feelings of almost constant upheaval all added up.

The United Nations had declared the 1980s as the decade for women, and my first role in my new job was to support the logistics for an international conference on equality, development, and peace in Copenhagen, Denmark. The conference was held in 1980, kicking off the push for greater equality across countries and continents. It was an era when women were emerging from oppression. The women's movement was gathering momentum across the western world; women were coming together to demand autonomy over their bodies, to seek rights to fully contribute to society, and to have their voices and opinions heard in a world dominated and run by men. On reflection, women's equality is needed as much now – 40 years later – as it was when the women's movement began back in the 1980s.

I settled into life in the city and the challenges of work engulfed me; nevertheless, they also provided a much-needed diversion from the chaos of my personal life. The conference gave me a sense of purpose; it allowed me to contribute to the larger cause of women across the globe struggling to advance. I felt very privileged and grateful.

Working in the United Nations was exhilarating. However, my enthusiasm in starting my new job was quickly suppressed by the frenzied atmosphere surrounding the preparation of the conference. My boss was the executive officer and conference administrator, a pleasant enough Greek man, whose main priority – ironically – was to surround himself with adoring young women. Everything else came in second place, including his job. Still, we worked tirelessly – managing visas, making arrangements for travel and hotel rooms, and confirming documentation for hundreds of attendees from all over the world.

As the conference drew near, I contemplated my future. I knew that spending a month in Copenhagen and leaving Dana in the hands of people I didn't know very well was not a viable option. In the frenzy of preparation, I kept a brave face, pushing forward. But I also knew I needed to explore other opportunities that would allow me to find a better balance between my personal life and my professional aspirations. The unpredictability of my past had shaped me, but I refused to let it define my future. I knew I needed to think carefully about planning a life that would be sustainable.

In the meantime, working in the United Nations was a totally new adventure, where celebrities and world leaders came through its doors – to make speeches, negotiate peace deals, or to receive guidance and advice on policy.

Not long after I started my new job, Pope John Paul II was scheduled to address the United Nations General Assembly. He was the first-ever Polish pope, having been elected in October 1978. I was so proud that one of my own countrymen had been elevated to such a high position and that he symbolized a shining beacon of peace in the world. Having only spent a short time working in the United Nations, I felt a flood of gratitude to have a once-in-a-lifetime opportunity to even be in the presence of this holiest of men.

One of my new colleagues, Shirley, recognized that as a Polish-born woman, I felt extra enthusiasm about the event. She worked her magic and sourced a ticket for me for the pope's address. In the days leading up to the visit, I was beside myself with excitement and anticipation. It was a dream that was on the verge of becoming a reality. The prospect of being in the presence of the pope, particularly one hailing from Poland, filled me with a profound sense of awe and reverence.

Although I had a ticket for the main event, a woman who worked in the same office grabbed another ticket from Shirley's hand that was for the visitors' section. She generously included me as part of the group of enthusiastic colleagues who would witness the pope's entrance into the United Nations visitors' area.

I could feel my heart pounding in my chest when His Holiness entered the building. I was the tallest woman in the group, dressed in an off-white suit, and as Pope John Paul II and his entourage walked in, we locked eyes. It was as if he had me in his sight and was heading straight toward me; however, within a split-second, he was guided in another direction and toward the dignitaries who were gathered to receive him.

I was nothing short of crestfallen, and could not hide the disappointment reflected on my face. An assistant in the entourage noticed my disappointment, and came over to console me; I was very appreciative of the gesture. Luckily, the ticket that Shirley secured for me was to attend the speech in the General Assembly Hall, giving me a second opportunity to see the pope.

For an organization that was so accustomed to having world leaders walk through its doors every day of the week, it was really unusual to witness UN staff lining up as if we were queuing for a huge rock concert, or to gain access to New York's famous nightspot, Studio 54.

We waited patiently in line for hours, joking and laughing, forging bonds with colleagues with whom we would not normally cross paths. We all shared the excitement of the momentous event. Finally, we made our way into the great hall, taking our seats as the intensity and the buzz of noise rose higher in the hall, turning the chatter and laughter into an electrifying atmosphere.

If you could bottle the mood that was in the hall that day, you would have it in your power to solve all of humanity's ills. I was seated in the middle of the 10th row, with a premium view of the podium. The General Assembly hall was at full capacity, and as the pope entered and approached the podium, a hushed silence fell.

His speech began; each word he uttered held immense weight. The pope's address, among other things, acknowledged the universal charter of the United Nations in fighting injustices and bringing peace. I felt so proud to work for this international organization. Midway through the address – very unexpectedly – a woman holding a baby walked up to the podium. The pope stopped his speech and blessed her baby.

I was spellbound to be in the presence of this holy man. As if I was hypnotized and with no control over my actions, I made my way out of the 10th row, asking to be excused by the others sitting in the row. I found myself walking towards the podium, much to the shock of my colleagues, the security officers – and myself. Step by step, I made my way up the aisle, looking at my feet, and asking myself, *What on earth am I doing?* I was making an absolute spectacle of myself, but I just could not stop.

My brain was pleading with my body to sit down – but there was another force, moving my body, that had other plans. I could not believe what was happening. I was a rookie, having only worked at the United Nations for several months. The UN secretary-general, heads of state, ambassadors, and the highest-ranking UN staff members were all present in the hall – and there I was, standing alone, facing one of the most famous and holiest of men in the world, Karol Józef Wojtyła, Pope John Paul II.

The area where the pope was speaking was roped off; I was standing just outside the rope. A security guard took my arm, trying to nudge me to return to my seat. But in the meantime, the kindly member of the pope's entourage who had previously consoled me approached me again and took my hand. He indicated that I didn't need to follow the security officer's instructions.

Blessing by Pope John Paul II at the United Nations

Just as the pope was finishing his speech, my hands began to rise above my head. He turned, looking me in the eye, and smiled – as he too reached his hands up and out toward me. My hands kept going up in the air; the security guard lifted the rope to allow me to walk right up to Pope John Paul II.

As I walked to the podium, I bowed my head and spoke a few words in Polish, telling him how honored I was to be able to greet my fellow country-man. To my astonishment, the Pope extended his hands over my head. He bestowed his blessing on me as I kissed his papal ring.

I almost started an international incident as the UN staff erupted with joy, rushing towards the pope, also hoping to receive his blessing.

As the staff surrounded His Holiness, security moved in to take control. Walking back to my seat, I felt overwhelmed by the magnitude of the surreal experience. It was a type of catharsis. It was as if the pope acknowledged and released me from the pain and suffering I had experienced. I couldn't hold back the tears of joy that streamed down my face. His blessing was a gift, a moment that is still so entrenched in my mind that I can seek it out and replay it whenever life presents great challenges. I felt an extraordinary sense of gratitude; a real awareness of endless possibility and optimism slowly began to heal my complicated past.

When I got back to the office, many of my colleagues who had seen the whole thing on UN television began to touch my arms as if to channel the Pope's blessing into themselves and their families. It wasn't until the next day – as I considered just how many celebrations of the Mass the Pope had con-ducted and how many thousands of people had traveled to see him – that I realized what a special moment I had experienced.

Moving Up

As the conference in Denmark grew closer and planning became more intense, I was working 12-hour days and weekends to complete the amount of tasks that landed on my desk. In the 1980s, there was no talk about work-life balance, and I began running on empty due to the stress of the impossible workload. I was certainly not meeting any minimum standard for a balance of work and home life, and I felt so guilty that I did not have sufficient time with Dana. I was torn between my career and my duty as a mother, and I was wracked with guilt because of my own history.

It was coming up to the end of 1979 and a new decade was about to begin. I decided that I needed to sort out the imbalance in my life. I went to the UN personnel unit to check the vacancies, and spotted an opening for the United Nations Population Fund, (known as UNFPA) in the Office of the Executive Director. I decided to contact the executive officer and met with him before making an application. After the interview I was offered the job, but had my doubts about accepting it, as it seemed to be far less challenging than the position I was in. However, my commitment to ensure that Dana would have the attention and love that I so missed in my own childhood saw me taking up the offer. The hours were better regulated, and there were opportunities to leave at a regular time when the director was traveling. It also meant that I would be around on weekends, and there for Dana in the mornings, packing her lunch and seeing her off to school.

Within a few months I was on the move again, within UNFPA, when I transferred to work for the second-in-command of the Information and External Relations Division. I was assigned to work alongside Jeannie, a real go-getter and a great boss. A tall, classy woman, she commanded respect and loyalty – and she got it, in spades. All of her staff were aware that if they brought an issue to her attention, it would be dealt with in a fair and just manner. Jeannie was a hard worker, but knew how to enjoy life and had a great sense of humor. She was someone I admired, and I loved working under such a highly competent woman. I learned so much and increased my knowledge of the complicated systems and policies of the UN. Jeannie and I soon became not only good colleagues, but also steadfast friends, and our friendship has remained strong over the intervening decades.

Jeannie's appreciation of my hard work paid dividends. Because she had no insecurities about her own ability, she lavished praise where it was due. She must have praised my work at higher levels, because before long, the division's director requested that I work in his office as his administrative assistant. It was a big step up for me, and I welcomed the learning curve and the new responsibilities that came with it. The job was still based in New York, but there was travel involved. I was entrusted with the preparation and management of all the conferences that came under the director's purview. I was happy to be in the position; I dealt with challenges and tasks that proved to benefit from my skill set. Ultimately, my new role would take me to far-flung corners of the globe.

In 1984, an international conference on population was to be held in Mexico City, which marked a new beginning for me. This was the second international UN-led conference that looked at population movements, bringing together some of the finest academics from across the globe to discuss and make recommendations on the mass movement of people. The conference looked at how the movement of people impacted the social and economic trajectories of individual countries. The conference's resulting recommendations influenced governments' planning and policies relating to agriculture, transport, education, health, and job creation, among other topics.

The logistics associated with this type of conference were massive, with each of the 147 participating countries sending several delegates. And then, there were also the researchers and academics from participating organizations. The attendance was upwards of 1,000 people – so, juggling flights, arranging hotel accommodations, and setting up visas were the central challenges. In addition, we had to have contingency plans for unforeseen circumstances, like illnesses and missed flights. It all required careful strategic planning.

Another requirement was to handle all the documentation that was required for a successful conference: accreditation, transcription of speeches, and providing enough interpreters for the various languages that would require translation. It took months of planning and late nights in the office, poring over each detail to ensure everything ran smoothly. These conferences were held on a regular basis and saw me travel to Barcelona, Spain, in 1986, back to Mexico in 1987, and then to Geneva, Switzerland, in 1988. In 1989, I had the opportunity to work in Amsterdam for a conference on populations in the 21st century. The job was "full-on" and I was enjoying every single moment.

Rediscovering Bonds

I became more established in New York with Dana. We moved from the shared house into a reasonably-sized apartment just a couple of blocks away. Teresa settled into married life with her husband Chester in Philadelphia. Being the artistic one in the family, she worked in a flower store, creating arrangements. She also took up painting as a hobby.

The other half of my family, Joanna and Ela, still lived in Poland. Ela was juggling her two young children, a husband and her job, while Joanna was enjoying student life. She was attending the University of Krakow, making the most of the opportunity to study while enjoying a certain amount of freedom.

My new apartment was more spacious than anywhere else I had lived, so I invited Joanna to come to New York. By that time, 1980, my Polish had improved considerably, so when Joanna arrived our communication was seamless. We developed an effortless bond; nowhere near as fraught as the relationship between Teresa and me.

Joanna paid attention to Dana and the pair became very close. It brought me great joy to see my daughter and her aunt forming such a strong relationship. We had a wonderful month together. In my free time, we covered the tourist trails and viewed famous landmarks: the Empire State Building, the United Nations, and all the other sights that make up New York, New York! We took trips on the weekend with Dana to the zoo, and ferry rides to places like Staten Island, Ellis Island and the Statue of Liberty. We had great fun hunting for bargains at stores such as Macy's, Bloomingdale's and Bergdorf Goodman.

Joanna was impressed with the vibrancy of the city; but after a month, she took refuge in Teresa's less crowded apartment in Philadelphia. However, Joanna would regularly return to New York for weekends, and it was always a pleasure to see her come through the door.

On one of those visits back to New York, a Polish friend introduced Joanna to Jacek, thinking they would be a perfect match. Jacek was also a Polish immigrant, albeit one that held a green card work permit. It wasn't long before they began dating, and within a year of arriving in the US, Joanna too had married.

Jacek was already living in New York, and once he and Joanna married, they moved into the same apartment building where Dana and I lived. I had not lived that close to family since I lived with my grandma in Krasne.

Joanna was a very quick learner; within no time at all, she had perfected English. It became difficult to detect a Polish accent anywhere in her speech. I paid for her to take typing classes, and once she had her work permit, she secured a job in a bank as a teller. Joanna was lucky to have two sisters on the lookout for her, and it made her integration and assimilation in the US a lot easier than it had been for me or Teresa. It was also a comfort to both Joanna and me to live in the same building and be neighbors. We were able to hook up on weekends and go out for coffee and lunches – sometimes hosting dinners in each other's apartments. We became close – and even more important to me, Dana became close to her aunt. Watching them interact was a real joy.

In 1985, Dana was 11 years old and growing fast. She also was curious about her family members that remained behind in Poland. I felt that she needed to meet and get to know her extended family, so I took her on her first trip to Poland.

We had a stopover in England, where we stayed with my dear friend Shirley. She had resigned from the United Nations and lived in Battersea, a suburb of London. It was my first time in London, and we were excited to see the sights of that great city. Dana and I did all the tourist things: Madame Tussaud's Museum, Buckingham Palace, the Tower of London, Harrods department store. Then, we walked the length of Oxford Street and through the streets of Chelsea – which was the center of London fashion – followed by rides in a red double-decker bus and a London taxi. During our visit, we also criss-crossed the city on the famous London "Tube." It was a packed four days as we soaked up English culture and history before catching our short flight to Poland.

Throughout her childhood, I had told Dana stories about my mother, grandmother, and the other family members we had on the other side of the

Atlantic Ocean. I would also tell her about our struggle to live in a communist country, and about the remoteness of where we lived. But there's nothing quite like seeing things for yourself. The premise of the trip for Dana was to meet the Polish side of her family, and for her to explore and connect with her roots.

We stayed with Ela in her home, where Dana met her cousins Adam and Ewa for the first time. They had fun trying to interpret each other's languages, and Dana quickly picked up a good smattering of Polish as a result of hanging out with her cousins. We visited Henrik and his family in Krakow, where Dana met yet another cousin. Uncle Marian had passed by then, but we went to meet with Aunt Helena, who was delighted to finally meet Dana. I felt very blessed that my family could meet the joy of my life and get to know her.

I was happy that two of my sisters had found partners in the States and that they had each made a life for themselves. However, their entry into the US had not been entirely the most legal way to enter the country. Because they had taken such a circuitous route toward citizenship, by the time I invited Ela to visit us in the States, the US embassy in Warsaw had other ideas about her coming here. My plans for a full reunion were soon scuttled as Ela's visa application was rejected. The reason given by the embassy was that Teresa and Joanna had stayed on beyond their holiday visas and settled in the US through marriage. I imagine that based on our track record, the US government wasn't betting that Ela would actually return to Poland. Achieving the dream of a reunion of all four sisters felt distant and insurmountable.

I had overcome many things in my life, so the matter of a visa refusal was miniscule in comparison to the other hurdles I had faced in my 30 years on the earth. It was still my deepest wish to have our family reunited for a celebration of our survival and reconnection. Ela was happy in Poland with her children; Joanna and her husband were blessed with twins – Agnes and Sebastian, born in 1993 (homegrown cousins for Dana). Teresa was childless, by choice. I just wanted to bring my siblings together, to stand in one place for a joyous celebration and to remember the people who loved us and had so much influence on shaping the people we became. We had not been in the same room all together since the night that Grandma, Uncle Henrik and Aunt Helena had discussed our future and subsequent separation.

I had gained a lot of confidence working at the United Nations, and had acquired a great understanding of government systems and how things worked. When I was in Poland with Dana, I made an appointment to see the ambassador of the United States consulate in Warsaw. I hoped to convey a little of the trauma our family had experienced and the long-term effect it had on our lives. I felt it was important to tell my story – our story – of separation and struggle, and also of our persistence and determination to find each other again. My aim was to appeal to the ambassador's humanity and empathy, and to overturn the previous visa refusal.

As I sat down with the ambassador, I looked her in the eyes and pleaded with her to read the letter I had written to the embassy, and then to let me know if the decision to refuse Ela's entry to the US was final. I also produced the original letter that Ela had sent to me after we had found each other. It was the letter that eventually reached me and highlighted the distress of our family's story, decades of separation, and our overwhelming desire to be together again.

The weight of my words hung in the air as I handed the ambassador the letter. As she read Elzbieta's heartfelt words, tears clouded her eyes, and I could sense that the depth of emotion in the letter resonated with her. It was not just a simple family story, but a representation of the unbreakable bond between sisters and the power of rekindling family ties. After a few moments of reflection, the ambassador made an exceptional – and unusual – decision to overrule the previous visa rejection and grant Elzbieta the opportunity to be a part of our long-awaited family reunion.

The ambassador's words filled me with a sense of complete happiness. A dream that seemed so far out of our reach was, at last, about to come true. Sisters, separated by time and distance, would finally be reunited as one family. The thought of all four of us coming together – the laughter, the shared stories, and the love that had transcended years – brought immense contentment to me. As Dana and I boarded the plane back to New York, I felt assured that my steadfast perseverance and love for my family could overcome any hurdle.

Once Ela's visa arrived, we began planning for her three-week trip. Her husband Henrik remained at home to look after their young children, who were still in school. When her plane landed at JFK, I was beside myself with excitement. I waited for my eldest sister to come through immigration; to finally have my dearest sister in my home with our other two sisters was beyond my wildest dreams. I welcomed her in the arrival hall with a huge hug – such a different scenario than what I experienced when I arrived in the US as a young child.

We returned to my home in Queens, where Dana was waiting to greet her aunt. That evening, Teresa and Joanna joined us at home, and we proceeded to stay up all night. We laughed, we drank, we cried, we reminisced, we remembered, we celebrated; and as the dawn came, we finally fell asleep.

Reunion – Ela, Teresa, Joanna and Krysia

Poor Ela just could not stop the tears, but they were tears of joy and hope. Over the next three weeks, Ela also visited Teresa's home in Philadelphia and stayed with her for a few days. Dana was on school holiday, so when Ela returned to New York City, Dana was able to be a tour guide for her while I worked. They weaved their way around the city to see the sites that Ela had only glimpsed in movies on the TV.

Ela had arrived with a suitcase full of our favorite food from Poland. During her few weeks with Dana and me, Ela's food suitcase was emptied of those treats and put to good use. She cooked our favorites: *pierogi, nalesniki, bigos,* and *placki.* We also treated Ela to some good old American food – hamburgers and hot dogs – and many ethnic foods that came to the US through immigrants like us. I think Ela was most excited and impressed when she saw the sheer choice and variety of available foods in the supermarket – and the 12 cashiers lined up to check out customers. When she returned to Poland, her suitcases would be filled once again, but this time with clothes and chocolates for the twins and her husband.

I continued to struggle with reconciling my two identities, but work provided a distraction, a reprieve from the chaos that had consumed me for so long. Work gave me a focus away from my personal life, and allowed me to think about other things that were going on in the world. The office became my refuge, a place where I could immerse myself in tasks, and surrounded by colleagues from the four corners of the globe. For the most part, my colleagues were like a small, supportive family, and I cherished the camaraderie and the solid friendships that were formed at work.

My job provided the stability I yearned for, but I still worried about my duties as a mother. I could not shake the feeling that I had neglected Dana while pursuing personal healing and professional success. I felt guilty that I could not provide her with the attention she needed, and my absences due to work commitments were affecting her development – especially her schoolwork. On the other side of the coin, I was a single mother and I depended on my job to provide for Dana's material needs. However, I felt that my precious daughter deserved better, and I was torn between my responsibilities as a mother and my own internal demons that I just couldn't shake.

Even so, we had some great times together. Dana loved visiting me at the office. It brightened up everyone's day to hear her laughter ringing through the workplace; she would announce herself at colleagues' desks with a smile and twinkle in her eye. There were times, though, when Dana missed school days, which was reflected in her schoolwork and grades. That was something I just couldn't ignore.

I thought long and hard about the situation, and weighed the options. Eventually, I came to the conclusion that it was time for Mike to take on some of the parenting responsibilities. Dana was Mike's only child, so there was no reason or excuse for him to not step up to the plate. I knew I had to consider what was best for Dana, even if it meant making sacrifices. I believed that our daughter might find more emotional support through the stability of living with her father, and I would continue to do whatever it took to ensure her happiness and well-being.

I reached out to Mike, who was still living in Philadelphia. In fairness, it did not take much convincing for him to agree that Dana should move in with her dad. Dana and Mike always had an excellent relationship – he never forgot her birthday, with gifts and cards arriving in the mail. When she went to live in Philadelphia with Mike, I continued to support her financially and emotionally as best as I could. I would call several times a week; and if Dana was not home, I would get updates from Mike. He not only had her interests at heart, but also agreed that her schooling was important to ensure she had a good education.

For me, the separation was heart-wrenching, but I prayed that I was making the right choice for her future. At every break, holiday weekend, or school vacation she would travel to New York and we would spend time together. I missed her around our home so much, especially when I came back from work each evening to an empty apartment. The times we spent together were very precious and I eagerly waited for each holiday to come along.

I had shared my backstory with close friends, who understood some of my angst and could sympathize with my situation. One friend thought I would benefit from professional counseling. He believed it would be a good idea to see a psychiatrist who could help me process the trauma I had suffered, and possibly allow me to find peace of mind. A friend of his highly recommended a doctor he had seen – the psychiatrist had a practice on 52nd Street and First Avenue in Manhattan.

This man specialized in treating adults who had experienced childhood trauma, so I made an appointment with his office. I had high expectations; I was prepared to put a lot of effort into taking control of my life and to find that inner peace that was so elusive. I took time off of work, and with no time to change from my work clothes, I arrived dressed as I would in the office, like the professional I was.

When I arrived, the office was more like a four-star hotel. It had dark wall panels and carpets that were so plush that footprints left marks with each step. The doctor was one of the most respected psychiatrists in the city, and I was prepared to be honest about the hurt, disappointment, and sadness I felt; how my past oozed into each day of my life. I wanted advice and answers on how I could reframe and process my past, in order to move on.

He was an older gentleman in a very expensive suit and rose to greet me before settling into his chair. I sat opposite him with a coffee table between us; a box of tissues was placed on top of the table. He opened his mouth, and after a short discussion, one of the questions he asked me was, "What kind of sex dreams do you have at night?" I could not fathom how such a question could even be relevant to my struggles.

I was shocked and totally disheartened that this man, with all his knowledge and prestige, could think of nothing else other than *sex*. Where was the relevance of the question? I left his office feeling even more lost and disillusioned, convinced that no one could begin to comprehend the depth of my pain. It was a weird encounter, and it made me question the validity of wanting to seek professional help. I did promise myself, however, that – to the best of my ability – I would push all the dreadful memories into the recess of my mind and move on with life.

I returned back to the hustle and bustle of the Daily News Building on 42nd Street in New York, where UNFPA had recently moved its offices, and I delved into a frenzy of work. We were preparing for an upcoming international conference on population in Mexico City. There was terrific energy in the building, and the new environment brought about a renewed verve and enthusiasm in the staff to pull together and get through the tasks ahead.

I was grateful for the diversion of a significantly increased workload, and I was committed to rising to the occasion.

My boss, a seasoned professional with a steely demeanor, decided to make an early trip to Mexico City to oversee the conference site and confirm security arrangements. I was assigned to join him; I was to provide administrative support for a full year – before, during and after the conference. We arrived at the sprawling conference site that would soon host over 1,000 participants from all across the world, and an international media contingent consisting of more than 2,000 journalists as well as camera crews.

We worked morning, noon and night to ensure that the conference attendees would have the necessary tools for a successful event. But the demanding workload and constant pressure began taking its toll on my health. On the morning of the conference, everything was running smoothly, but I began to feel incredibly weak. Before I knew it, and without any warning, I collapsed into a heap. Everyone rushed over to assist me, and at least one person with a cool head had the good sense to take me to the conference doctor. I was diagnosed with hypoglycemia.

I could barely speak or move; my blood sugars were so low that I simply could not function. My condition was brought on largely by the enormous stress I had been under. The doctor admitted me to the hospital, where I was put on intravenous glucose to return my blood sugars to acceptable levels. I spent the night in the hospital and was released the next day – I saw it as just a setback in my schedule. I was too stubborn to allow the episode to get in the way of the job I had set out to do.

I returned to work; however, it was not long before I was the center of attention again, with yet another dramatic collapse. The second time, I was admitted to a hospital in Mexico City – for just a day – and was released again. Nevertheless, on the day I was to leave Mexico after the conference, I was directed to check into the hospital. They would not allow me to fly out of Mexico until I was certified healthy enough to return to New York.

I loved my work in the United Nations – the interaction with people from around the globe, the discovery of commonalities, and the forming of new friendships. I got to know people whom I would never have had an opportunity to meet – let alone become friends with – had it not been for my job. I was intrigued by the stratosphere of power and diplomacy, with opportunities to interact with presidents, kings, queens, prime ministers, and diplomats.

The central mission of the United Nations intrigued me – the maintenance of international peace and security. Each year, when the General Assembly gathers in New York and dignitaries come to participate, the city comes to a standstill as dignitaries are brought in to participate in that annual event. On a world stage, leaders discuss international events, poverty, climate change, conflict, human rights, elections, equality, and any policies that could help communities and countries. I was eager to make my own contribution to the UN mandate in whatever small way that presented itself.

As a result of my hard work as well as good fortune, UNFPA allowed me to step out of my usual role and participate in the 40th anniversary celebration of the founding of the United Nations in 1985. The streets around the UN building buzzed with anticipation; the main event would be televised across the world.

International Forum, Amsterdam, The Netherlands

During that time, Dana was traveling from her dad's house to visit me in New York during holiday breaks and long weekends. And whenever school let out for the summer, Dana would come to stay with me for two months.

So, each June, I would reserve a hotel on the Jersey shore for at least a week or two. We cherished our walks along the boardwalk, the sun-soaked days on the beach, and all the precious moments reconnecting. In Manhattan, our summer adventures included exploring Central Park, dining at cafés on Central Park South, and going to Broadway shows. We would wander through Soho and Greenwich Village, savoring our favorite Manhattan eateries. Those times together were filled with joy – and the occasional mother-daughter conflicts. Still, each moment was memorable.

Dana in Central Park

Exploring the World

Up to that time, most of my travel consisted of trips to Central America and Europe. Other than flying to Poland, which became my regular go-to destination for personal travel, I had gone to Spain, the Netherlands, France, Italy, Switzerland, and several other European countries to attend conferences.

In the years since I had moved to the director's office in UNFPA, my former boss Jeannie was assigned to the Philippines and was living in its capital, Manila. The Philippines, an archipelago of more than 7,500 islands, is part of the Ring of Fire (an area where the majority of the seismic and volcanic activity in the world occurs). The country encounters some of the most powerful typhoons each year, as well as regular earthquakes, tsunamis and volcanic eruptions. While there was great wealth in the country at the time, it was accompanied by huge levels of corruption among the ruling elite. Those were the days when the president's wife, Imelda Marcos, became renowned for her wardrobe – she boasted of thousands of pairs of shoes, while millions of people lived in abject poverty. The poverty was especially felt by women and children; there was a general lack of investment in women's health.

Jeannie's position as the Philippines' representative of UNFPA was to ensure that the agency was working with the government to help improve the country's maternal mortality rates.

The Philippines are unusual in terms of religious belief. Once occupied by the Spanish, whose colonization bequeathed the Catholic religion to the majority of the population, the nation is surrounded by countries that have other dominant religions. Indonesia has the biggest Muslim population in the world; Thailand, Cambodia and Vietnam have a strong Buddhist following, and the Japanese mainly follow the Shinto religion and Buddhism.

At the end of the 19th century, the Spanish left the Philippines when the US occupied the islands. The US used the Philippines as a strategic base because of its location at the center of the Pacific Ocean; however, the United States' 48-year occupation ended in 1946, just a year after the end of World War II. Nevertheless, the US influence left some positive changes, especially in education, where the independent Filipino government kept the American-style system. American culture also seeped into sports, manifesting in the Filipinos' love of basketball, so much so that there are nightly news updates regarding the various basketball leagues.

Jeannie's three-year assignment was coming to an end when she invited me for a visit to experience Asia for the first time. In true Jeannie fashion, she showed me all parts of the Philippines, warts and all. I accompanied her on visits to the UNFPA projects around the slums of Manila; there was no imagination required to see the levels of poverty experienced by millions of Filipinos. Many were living in overcrowded conditions; yet they traveled each day into the upmarket areas to work in the service industry as maids, waiters, cleaners and drivers. These days, Filipinos also work in the many call centers across Manila, providing support for global firms and responding to queries from individuals in far-flung countries.

I watched these young men and women coming out of their tenements; they were turned out with beautifully-ironed and spotlessly-clean clothes. It would have taken a huge effort for someone living in such conditions to dress so meticulously for work each day; yet, these Filipinos presented themselves with pride and dignity.

Outside Manila, we visited the island of Boracay, setting off in a twin-engine, four-seat plane and then traveling by tricycle and boat to this slice of paradise in the South China Sea. There was no electricity on the island, which made living conditions difficult for the local community. Accommodation was basic, but comfortable. Meals were cooked on a grill or open fire and water was taken from the local rivers. The rivers also provided the water for a cool shower in the mornings. A huge positive aspect of having no electricity meant that sitting outside at night by the campfire – without artificial light pollution – revealed the majestic magnitude of the night skies. It was especially wonderful to see the Milky Way so distinctly.

With Jeannie, going to Boracay Beach, The Philippines

I loved my job with UNFPA, but I had a thirst for adventure. Upon my return to New York, I decided that I wanted to experience other cultures and see what lay outside my comfort zone. The added bonus would be for me to contribute in some small way to advancing democracy and to the mandate of the United Nations to help bring peace to the world.

In the late 1980s and early '90s, I harbored a strong desire to join a peacekeeping mission, particularly during Namibia's transition to independence from South Africa. Despite preparing all necessary paperwork, I withdrew my application because I received advice that I might lose my United Nations post. A few years later, a similar opportunity arose with the Cambodian peacekeeping mission, but my responsibilities with the UNFPA executive board in Geneva precluded my participation. My aspirations in that direction seemed to dwindle until a fateful lunch with friends at work. It was another "sliding door moment" – a colleague joined the table, and as the conversation progressed, she casually mentioned that there was a UN effort to recruit election observers for the upcoming elections in Angola.

When I returned to my office, I called personnel and set up a meeting for the following day. In 1992, there weren't too many volunteers looking to go into a civil war environment to secure fair and democratic elections, and I'm sure that the personnel executive processing my application was more than a little perplexed at my enthusiasm.

Once I secured the temporary assignment for the Angola elections, I then had to negotiate with my three supervisors for special leave so I could embark on the mission. I presented my case – I turned on the charm and assured the directors that my responsibilities in the office would not be ignored while I completed the mission in Angola.

It was an onerous process to get my travel leave approved; it occurred to me that there must be less bureaucracy involved to have a new pope elected! Yet, at the end of two months, I began preparation for the two-week trip – my first time to an African country. But then, personnel put another obstacle in my way, when I was informed that I was required for two months in Angola – not two weeks. I braced myself again and went on another major charm offensive with my supervisors. With renewed persistence, I managed to convince them of my ability to continue with my office duties for two months while serving in the role of election observer.

By that time in my life, Dana had grown accustomed to traveling back and forth between Mike's home and mine on holidays, on long weekends, and during summer school vacations. As she got older, Dana no longer wanted to spend the full two months of summer in Manhattan, preferring instead to spend time with her dad and school friends. Nevertheless, our time together remained special. When she came to New York, I would take her shopping for clothes or makeup and anything else she might need. Often, when work demanded my presence, Dana would accompany me to the office, where she would offer to sharpen pencils or help out with the printer (at which she became an expert). Her beautiful smile brightened everyone's day at the office, making the memories even more cherished for both of us.

Angola

Going to Angola was a first for many things for me – it was my first African country, my first mission to the field, and my first time to witness the horrifying effects of war. Angola encompasses twice the landmass of Texas or France, and when I arrived there was little or no infrastructure. Roads were nonexistent, and drinking water sources, sewage systems, schools, health centers, and hospitals were damaged. Most everything was beyond repair.

Ultimately, the infrastructure could be repaired and replaced – albeit at a great cost. But the suffering – the cost to human life – was immeasurable. To this day, Angola remains one of the most land-mined countries in the world, with nine million mines across vast tracts of land. Famously, Princess Diana was filmed in Angola while witnessing the work of the mine clearance teams, which spotlighted the dreadful damage that mines can have on communities. Decades after the mines were planted, their effect on people and the environment remains. Almost always, the presence of mines leaves farmland – and ergo, produce – unavailable for ordinary folk. The lack of access to agricultural land in Angola reminded me of how lucky we were in Krasne after World War II, where at least we had the means to grow our own food.

Of course, the damage caused by land mines is mostly felt by civilians, who are either killed or maimed. Life-changing injuries caused by exploding mines usually involves amputation[1]. Despite Angola's rich oil reserves and potential revenue, the poverty rates among its citizens remain abysmal, with 30 percent of the population still living below the poverty line – and life expectancy rates are 60.4 years for men and 64.7 years for women[2].

I was the only white female on the flight into the capital city, Luanda. Most of the passengers were businessmen hoping to make a quick buck from the oil industry or by rebuilding the country's infrastructure. I was advised that the United Nations had faxed my date and time of arrival in Luanda to contacts there, so it had not occurred to me that I would need to make a hotel reservation. But as I overheard the men's conversations on the flight, making their deals and arranging meetings at various hotels, it occurred to me: *What if no one is there to pick me up at the airport?* I had no hotel reservation, so my only hope would be to follow the passengers and see where they were staying, and then try to get a room at the same place.

The airport was a dank, dirty, and dreary place, and I – with my two huge suitcases – followed the businessmen out into the arrival hall. My eyes scanned the unfamiliar surroundings and I began to absorb my new environment. I arrived at the concourse, and while I was not expecting a brass band, I did expect to be met by at least a single person from the United

Nations who cared enough not to leave me on the curbside in such a dangerous environment.

Then, out of the corner of my eye, I spotted the United Nations flag on a Jeep that was about to pull away. Dropping my bags on the sidewalk, I ran toward the car, screaming, "Stop, stop, stop, I'm UN staff!" Lady Luck was shining down on me that day – the Jeep stopped, and I identified myself to the driver, who told me he was expecting me the following day.

On the way to the UN camp, the vehicle cruised through the streets of Luanda. I gazed out the window and took in the sights, sounds, and unique smell of the unfamiliar city. Women carried babies on their backs and balanced huge bundles on their heads, which contained food and goods that they were selling. Men huddled in circles around small fires, smoking and drinking coffee. There were deep craters in the roads, filled with muddy water; the driver skillfully negotiated his way around them. Buildings were crumbling down as if some mighty earthquake had struck everything in one swift blow. All of the devastation was the result of years of civil war – and yet, life went on as if it all was somewhat normal.

No one seemed to notice the men walking the streets with AK-47s, the weapon of choice, strung across their backs. The journey, even only up to that point, provided a glimpse into the complexities of Angola grappling with the aftermath of a brutal war.

The upcoming elections required a UN presence, partly for observation but mainly for peacekeeping. The fragile peace agreement negotiated between the warring parties arbitrarily broke down as the country grappled with its transition to democracy. Angola's reputation as a lawless and very dangerous country was well earned. My particular team was in Angola to document any discrepancies, such as fraudulent voting or vote-buying. We were aiming to make certain that a fair and transparent election took place.

The UN's love affair with acronyms continued in Angola, where the Angola Verification Mission was known as UNAVEM. The staff compound, Vila Espa, was located on the outskirts of Luanda. I was assigned to an 8-by-10-foot shipping container, a common form of accommodation in war zones where the UN was present. Amenities included a desk, a bed, a wardrobe – and in some cases, where the mission is well established – a bathroom. If you were not lucky enough to have your own bathroom, trips to one during the night could be fraught with hazards!

UN staff who spend a lot of time living in such containers often bring trinkets from home to decorate their living quarters. I have seen Afghan carpets and beautiful artwork from local artists decorating a container's interior, turning a drab, utilitarian piece of metal into a comfortable space resembling a home. But compound living can be stressful, and the compound can often be the target of disgruntled militants who like to take potshots or throw the odd rocket over the perimeter wall.

One of the more endearing aspects of compound living is the bonds and friendships that are formed. I feel that this naturally happened when the people there sought out others with similar aspirations. We put our trust in each other; we knew we would have to rely on our colleagues and staff to sometimes act in life-saving situations when the "manure hit the fan."

The big downside of living in a container is that they are not insulated. So, once the weather turns cold in winter, you can freeze; and then of course, metal holds heat, so summertime means that the containers turn into a furnace. It's rarely cold in Angola; so, with the scorching heat of the African sun, my container would become unbearably hot within five minutes. That left me little choice but to pull up a chair to sit outside, hoping for a breeze to help me cool down. My nearest neighbor was a Dutch police officer, and we became acquainted over the next few days while we waited to hear news of our assignments.

Going on mission in the UN required schmoozing with people in two different sections. One person was the information technology expert, as something almost always went wrong with a laptop. Or, there would be issues such as incompatibility among individual countries' operating systems. Befriending a techie in the IT section was always a good way to avoid stress.

The other important person that required schmoozing is the Movement Control (MovCon) person. The people who work in MovCon are in charge of transporting staff – and that includes travel by helicopters and small planes. I befriended Chino, who oversaw the manifest sheet for the supply plane – a Russian Antonov. Traveling by road was not a good option in Angola. For starters, there were few decent roads remaining – most were dirt tracks, and many tracks remained strewn with land mines. There was also the additional menace of armed rebels who continued to roam the bush, making kidnapping a real threat. The aircraft traversed across Angola, delivering staff, essential equipment, and medical supplies to duty stations.

While I waited to see what part of the country I would work in, I took the opportunity to read about – and visit – different regions in Angola. Chino gave me a heads-up one day when a flight had empty seats, which allowed me to visit the different polling station sites and observe the situation on the ground. My first stop took me north of Luanda, 250 kilometers away, to the town of Dondo. The town had a population of around 60,000, and the location of the UN regional office was perched on the top of a hill.

As we flew in, we could see women with huge plastic buckets on their heads, gathering at the riverbank to wash their families' clothes. In Dondo, fierce fighting during the war had displaced many of the townspeople; their homes were destroyed. Afterward, they found themselves living in camps under very basic conditions. There was no work available, so the men would buy *khat*, an evergreen shrub that is chewed to bring on a state of euphoria and stimulation. It's a common practice in many African countries, and people who chew the plant are easily identified by their stained yellow teeth. Chewing the plant's leaves over a period of time frequently leads to psychosis and unpredictability.

Russian Antonov supply plane, going to regional offices in Angola

I could feel the tension of the election officials. They were eager to show us the bullet holes in the walls after a disgruntled individual – who had most likely spent his day chewing *khat* – had climbed the hill and spent the evening randomly shooting off his AK-47.

Luena was our next stop, a city and municipality in eastern Angola and the administrative capital of Moxico province. At one time, it was one of the most land-mined places in Angola. The regional office or camp that we visited in Luena was more extensive than Dondo, with a lot more people working there. Because it had much better facilities, it could offer some semblance of normality and a relatively calm atmosphere.

Finally, we made our way to Saurimo. It is situated at more than 3,500 feet above sea level – so it doesn't have the same intensity of daytime heat as lower altitudes. Certainly, nights there were a good deal cooler. Saurimo is best known for its rich resources, including diamonds, agriculture and oil. Not only were locals displaced there, but it was also a big refugee hub due to civil unrest in the neighboring Republic of the Congo and the Democratic Republic of the Congo. Nevertheless, the camp in Saurimo was the most orderly we visited. It was well-managed and offered the promise of a successful assignment.

Un Camp in Saurimo

Each stop on our journey allowed us to see for ourselves the complexities in conducting an election that was corruption-free and fair. Our trip proved to be very worthwhile and constructive. Once we finished in Saurimo, we headed back to our base in Luanda. We spent six hours on the plane bent over on hard wooden seats, and I was so stiff after disembarking that it took me 10 minutes to be able to even stand up straight.

When living in dangerous conditions, there's a tendency to party hard, making the most of whatever free time comes at weekends. The day-to-day unpredictability led to really high stress levels, which could sometimes be like steam inside a pressure cooker. I had befriended Yvonne, another UN colleague, who in turn introduced me to a group of New Zealand military officers stationed on the compound.

In high spirits one weekend, we set out for dinner at a restaurant on the shore with a young captain as our driver. His youth and inexperience almost got us into deep trouble; in fact, it was such deep trouble that we almost never returned. Foolishly, he took a shortcut that led us onto some off-road driving, far from the usual route. We found ourselves driving along a desolate, isolated stretch; and before long, we arrived upon a figure in a military uniform standing in the middle of the track – with an AK-47 menacingly pointed at us.

It became obvious that our young driver had completed some training as we approached the rogue militant; he advised us to stay inside the vehicle, no matter what happened. Our chances of survival would be greatly enhanced if we remained together. My heart was almost jumping out of my chest and my stomach went into a knot with fear, but outwardly I remained calm. As we pulled up alongside the rebel and he put the gun near our driver's head, the smell of alcohol was overpowering. He slurred his words, demanding that we get out of the car. We attempted to reason with him, pleading to allow us to continue our journey, but he was adamant.

We kept joking with this drunk, armed and dangerous man, as the driver moved the car forward inch by inch. Finally, we had moved some distance and the captain shouted at us to hit the floor. He put his foot down on the gas pedal and no one looked back to see if the rebel had readied his AK-47 to take a potshot at us. I suspect that even if he had tried to fire at the car, he was too drunk to aim with any accuracy.

The friendships that were struck during adversity became a source of support and safety in the face of our unpredictable environment. The episode with the drunk rebel was a stark reminder of the hidden, unpredictable dangers that lurked in every corner in the aftermath of Angola's civil war.

I was lucky when I was assigned as the team leader in Saurimo. Saurimo was the most organized of the polling stations we had previously visited. As a UN electoral observer, my role was to travel to the towns and villages in the area to report on any discrepancies in the organizing phase of the election. Discrepancies could include insufficient space between booths, or lack of divisions in the booths to provide privacy for people to vote. There were no political posters allowed within a certain distance of a polling booth and such incidents needed to be reported. In some places, you could find politicians handing out money to voters to try and buy votes. And of course, on polling day, ballot boxes could go missing; or extra ballot boxes could appear out of nowhere, stuffed with fake ballots.

First, I had to find the towns and villages where the polling stations were located. Today, we can't seem to leave home without using the GPS on our phone. But back in 1992, we relied on the age-old tradition of noting landmarks: "...Continue for a mile, where you will find a tree on the right; then continue on as far as the ant hill on the left, and follow the track for another

800 yards when you come to a hut, where there's a dog who frequently sits on the roadside and barks at passing cars."

There were no tarmac roads in rural areas; we traveled the uneven mud tracks in a Jeep. Driving from towns to villages also presented a potential for grave danger. Diverting even a fraction off the "approved" track meant that there was a good chance we would end up in a minefield. Unexploded ordnance devices detonate with weight, so if a car happens to drive over a mine, the passengers would have little opportunity for survival, despite the armored plating.

Somewhere in rural Angola

Everyone in the car was on high alert as we moved from place to place. We were provided with a list of towns and villages in our area of responsibility. We needed to visit them before election day, to ensure that they had made adequate plans and so we could introduce ourselves. We met with the elders to explain our role, and made sure they had all the necessary equipment. We also answered any questions that they had. The meetings reassured the townspeople of our intention to facilitate free and fair elections.

Obtaining the approval of the elders was key to a successful mission. They guided us to the buildings designated for voting, and showed us how they had made structures such as the voting booths. The people we met along the way welcomed us as new friends, often inviting us to sit and eat with them – a true gesture of hospitality, sharing what little they possessed. As the weeks passed and we crisscrossed the rugged terrain, we would revisit the polling stations to confirm that all was in order for election day.

Elections in a war zone or postwar climate can always be tricky. Candidates from the vying political parties can coerce voters, threatening violence or paying poor people a few cents to buy their votes. When violence erupts, many of the female voters stay at home, fearing that fighting will get out of hand. And, starting violence in an area can often be used as a tactic to do just that – to intimidate voters into staying at home.

Despite such challenges, there was excitement, with the hope of more peaceful times ahead. As election day loomed, voters lined up, eager to cast their votes. I felt a deep sense of gratitude and privilege to witness each constituent's contribution through the election process – the freedom of choice that would provide a path toward a more promising future.

We were a team made up of myself, as leader; a UN Swedish military observer; and a Spanish captain who acted as a translator and the driver of our UN four-wheel drive vehicle. We set out to visit as many polling stations as we could fit in over a 24-hour period. The vehicle was laden with emergency supplies, two spare wheels, walkie-talkies (so we could communicate with our base), a medical first aid kit, and enough water to last us several days.

At one point, we arrived at a bridge that – having come under heavy bombing – was damaged and impassable. I made a decision for the team to walk the half-mile to the polling station, leaving our driver in the car to ensure it wasn't vandalized. We traveled up hills and down valleys, until our bones were shaken as if we had been traveling on the back of a mixologist making James Bond's favorite martinis – shaken, not stirred. We held up the UN flag to indicate our peaceful intentions and were welcomed to the village.

My electoral team (Swedish Military Observer and Spanish Captain)

Voting started at sunrise and finished at sunset; and once voting stopped, the count began, going through to the early hours of the morning. We selected count centers to visit during the night, observing and noting any signs of malpractice. It was too late to travel back to our base, so we pulled out the tents that were packed away in the trunk and took a few hours rest before returning to our compound.

I felt pleased to have completed a successful mission without incident. The office in New York was looking for my immediate return, so after a few days, I flew back to Luanda to confirm that my flight to New York was booked. Then, I returned to Saurimo to write up my report and pack my bags. In the meantime, the United Nations, along with the election commission, announced the results of the election – and not all the political parties were pleased. Within a short time, an angry crowd gathered outside our camp, letting us know in no uncertain terms what they thought of the results. The situation had the potential to become nasty, and it certainly was tense. Our security officer took control, and after some hours managed to calm the situation, allowing the team to exit and return to Luanda.

At the compound in the capital, we expected to debrief the people in charge; but word came from our security officer that I was to leave immediately. MovCon was ready and waiting at the gate; and I, along with some other colleagues, was speedily escorted to the airport with no explanation.

We were rushed through customs and immigration, and took off within 20 minutes of arriving at the airport. I watched Luanda disappear below through the window as we climbed into the skies. Once again, I had a stopover in Brussels; I appreciated the luxury of a comfortable bed and a decent hot shower in my hotel room.

I lay on the bed in my room and switched on the TV, scrolling through the channels until I came across CNN. The headlines made me sit up in shock as I realized why we had been rushed out of Angola. Once the election result was announced, violence had erupted, sending the country into outbursts of conflict. The losing party in the elections – none too pleased with the results, and determined to disrupt the democratic process – had descended into Luanda. They had begun to loot the stores and spray the streets with gunfire.

I felt relieved that I had managed to leave the country before the violence erupted, and grateful to be in the safety of a European city. But I was also devastated for the people who I met along the way and who were so hopeful of achieving democracy and peace in the lead-up to the elections.

Many of the election observers were left stranded in downtown Luanda, locked down in the UN compound. They were waiting for the violence to subside, so they could safely evacuate to the airport and leave the country. I was grateful that my return flight was confirmed and booked, allowing me to leave rather than remain trapped with the others in the chaos and miss more of my duties in New York.

While I was stationed in Angola, I had intermittent contact with Dana and her dad. I kept track of her progress, but I never fully informed her of any of the dodgy adventures I had experienced. Telephone connections were not very efficient and I was often frustrated when trying to call. I missed her dreadfully; and there were times we could only communicate by email.

When I returned to the States, it was good to catch up with Dana; and at the end of October 1992, she made the trip to New York so that we could reconnect. In the meantime, I resumed work at UNFPA and did my best to settle back into office life. But the taste for adventure was like an addictive drug – once I had that first sip, I just wanted more. I loved having to think on my feet, learning about new cultures and politics, making and bonding with new friends, as well as the opportunity to live life to the fullest.

By chance, I came across an opportunity to join the UN peacekeeping mission in Mozambique (designated with the acronym ONUMOZ), and looked at it as a great opportunity to do some good – as well as satisfy my taste for adventure. However, during the same period, the country of Somalia was experiencing difficulties – customary law temporarily collapsed, and civil war erupted in the absence of a central government.

Staffing the Somalia mission became a priority for the UN, and I discovered that colleagues who applied for positions in Mozambique had ended up in Somalia. This was in response to Somalia's "failed state" status, which made it necessary for the UN to set up a mission there with military observers. That was followed in 1993 with a peacekeeping mission. I needed to strategize to avoid ending up in Somalia; so I set about making contacts and reaching out to the key decision-makers.

I received good news in June 1993 – I was selected for the Mozambique mission. Once that was confirmed, I set about requesting a release from my New York post. I also needed to sublet my Manhattan apartment to help pay the rent. UNFPA thought that by ignoring my endless requests for release, I would give up and continue as usual, but they did not know me very well.

I put my apartment up for rent, and one of my first callers for viewing the place was from Ama Annan, who – along with her dad Kofi – came to see the apartment. They expressed interest in Ama renting it while I was out on mission. In 1993, Kofi Annan was the UN under-secretary-general in waiting, and the future sidekick to Boutros Boutros-Ghali, the secretary-general at the time. Ama was interested in speeding up the process of renting my place, and when she had not heard from me after a week, she made contact to know what date she could move in. So I sent a simple note to personnel, explaining that Kofi Annan's daughter was asking when I would be going on a mission, as she was waiting to move into my apartment. Quicker than you could say "Olympic gold medal sprinter," I was released to work in the Mozambique mission.

Mozambique

Mozambique is roughly as big as the combined areas of the US states of Colorado, New Mexico, and Utah, stretching along the Indian Ocean coast in east Africa from Cabo Delgado in the north past the capital city of Maputo in the south. The country gained independence from Portugal in 1975, after enduring 470 years of exploitation through oppressive rule and colonization.

Throughout Portuguese rule, the country was purged of its natural resources and wealth while no resources were returned back into the country. As a result, when Mozambique gained independence – encouraged by Cuba and the Soviet Union – they embraced Marxism.

In 1976, a geopolitical war broke out when troops from Zimbabwe (then known as Rhodesia) entered Mozambique to carry out operations against the Zimbabwe African Liberation Army, who had bases in Mozambican territory. The ensuing civil warfare displaced as many as four million people and resulted in the death of an estimated one million (from a population of 14 million) due to famine, poverty and disease.

By 1990, South Africa was moving towards a black, majority-controlled government and the Soviet Union had been disbanded. Despite its mineral wealth and opportunity for progress, the additional impact of violence in Mozambique continued to affect any economic development, discouraging foreign investment.

After a successful peace accord agreement in Rome, ONUMOZ was set up to support the peacekeeping mission for which I was recruited. The presence of the UN effectively ended the war, but sporadic violence continued to break out. And even as the advent of the 21ˢᵗ century loomed, there were as many as one million unexploded land mines along the country's trails and roads.

Political strife continued between the opposition Mozambique National Resistance (RENAMO) and the central government. The UN mission's primary goal was to facilitate the end of the Mozambican Civil War, which had lasted for over 15 years, and support the country's transition to a much-needed democratic nation that could guarantee peace and stability to its citizens.

Over the centuries, each colonizing nation came with an agenda, whether it was the Spanish in the Philippines, or the French in Angola and Senegal, or the English – who colonized so many countries that they boasted that the sun never set on their empire. The Portuguese were no different, colonizing Mozambique for its gold, spices, and cloth. In addition, Portugal valued Mozambique for its easy access to south Asia. As with all colonizers, Portugal's language and culture were forcefully imposed on the colony's population. Possibly the only positive outcome of Portuguese colonization was the charm of the colorful colonial buildings that made Maputo so vibrant. The city grew around the Indian Ocean coastline, offering my type of perfect climate with an energy and vitality that made me feel at home almost immediately. However, many of the buildings in the city were run-down and damaged from explosions during the war. With a busy work schedule, I, along with a colleague, booked into a local hotel that provided charming accommodations near our office. The room to which I was assigned was clean and comfortable, with appealing nearby restaurants that catered to international tastes.

Often when the United Nations sets up a mission in a country in a post-war scenario, there is insufficient office space, so the UN will take over a local hotel until there is a viable enough infrastructure to construct offices. In Maputo, the Ruvuma Hotel became our office. The hotel was basic and worn, but functional enough for us to carry out our mandate. The hotel owner was paid an agreed annual fee, and the bedrooms were converted to office space; there was no shortage of bathrooms for staff. I immersed myself in work, familiarizing myself with my new role and learning about the country's political situation. The little amount of free time we were afforded was spent getting to know Maputo and the rhythm of life there. Each day offered new opportunities to experience the rich culture, connect with locals, and witness the resiliency of Mozambicans.

The United Nations mandate is aspirational – its purpose is to strive for equality, equity and world peace – a truly noble pursuit. However, the organization is made up of individuals – good, bad and indifferent. Recruitment can result from friendships and networking, rather than meritocracy. When you come across a colleague who has risen through the ranks, but is incompetent, you end up carrying their workload. You know they didn't get the job on meritocracy; and it does not take much research to find out who their friends are. That can be very frustrating.

Every now and again, though, you will come across a leader with a brilliant mind and an aptitude for diplomacy. They will have both charisma and organizational skills. Setting up and leading a UN mission such as ONUMOZ requires a certain talent. The ability to speak to and support the government, while remaining knowledgeable about the issues that motivate the rebels, requires expertise. The word around the office was that an Iranian career diplomat, at the level of assistant secretary-general, was to be appointed as the United Nations deputy special representative of the secretary-general (DSRSG) to the mission in Mozambique.

Deputy Special Representative of the Secretary-General, Behrooz Sadry

My own supervisor spoke very highly of this new boss, Behrooz, who was known for his remarkable negotiation skills. The idea of getting such a well-known, prestigious diplomat to run the mission lifted staff morale, renewing a sense of purpose and optimism among us. While UN headquarters was in the process of organizing his credentials, the assistant secretary-general met with government leaders and visited our offices to introduce himself. I was struck by his gracious demeanor, good manners, and impeccable taste in clothes. He appeared every bit the quintessential diplomat, and I could not help but feel that his presence would have a positive impact on the mission. But it would be several more weeks before the administration nuances were complete and he could join the mission in Maputo.

Off to Bazaruto

In the meantime, a colleague in the procurement section mentioned that there was a spare seat on a small plane traveling to the Bazaruto archipelago, a group of six islands off the coast of southern Mozambique. Around a dozen of us took off one weekend in the chartered flight, landing on the main island.

The archipelago is renowned for pristine white sand beaches with coral reefs that protect rare marine animals. As many as 2,000 fish species, including whales and dolphins, can be found there. The wetland forests and grassland of the interior of Benguerra – the second-largest island in the archipelago – are home to many exotic bird species. I was struck by the lush environment in this slice of paradise, surrounded by crystal-blue water. It was a long weekend and we had no work; so, with the prospect of a carefree, work-free few days, we hit the bar after throwing our bags into our hotel rooms.

We were high on freedom and also somewhat "high" on the wonderful cocktails served at the bar; we went into full party mode. There were some men there dressed in their shorts with great polo shirts and tanned bodies, playing pool. They all looked as if they had stepped out of a TV advertisement for men's aftershave – and one, in particular, was even more handsome than the others.

In the lead-up to our mini-break, it had been a tough few weeks. The alcohol went straight to my head. Although I made a mental note of the gorgeous man at the bar, I was too tired and possibly a little too drunk to bother flirting with him in the early morning hours. So, I headed off to my room to savor the prospect of a night's sleep. The next day, there were no alarm clocks or wake-up calls except for the sun rising across the horizon and bathing the room in morning light. But the prospect of having a day free to do absolutely nothing encouraged most of us to stay in our rooms, nursing hangovers.

On the third day, some of the gang set out in a small, rented boat to explore the other islands, where they were able to snorkel. On their return, they were excited to describe how they had been swimming alongside the most beautiful sea creatures imaginable. I was sorry I had not taken the opportunity to go and observe the thousands of various multicolored marine animals in their natural habitat of pristine coral.

On the last day of our weekend trip, I was making the most of the remaining time on the island. I was stretched out on a sunbed when the very good-looking man that I had spotted playing pool that first evening appeared like a mirage shimmering in the African sun.

Stephan was a South African businessman from Cape Town, and he and his friends had been on a hunting expedition in Zimbabwe. He introduced himself, and asked if I would like to join him and his friends for lunch on the veranda overlooking the water.

He was very charming and engaging as the conversation flowed over lunch. Once we finished eating, I excused myself to make the most of the last few moments of uninterrupted sunshine that day. Stephan joined me, and we continued our conversation, turning the talk to the challenges facing Africa as well as the role of the United Nations.

My colleagues had returned from another boat trip and were packing up to head to the airport. Before I joined the taxi that would take us to the airport, Stephan and I shared a long, passionate kiss – out of view of my colleagues. It was like something out of the movie Casablanca with Lauren Bacall and Humphrey Bogart. We made plans to meet the next evening in Maputo by the piano bar at the Polana Hotel, a favorite place among expats.

I headed to the piano bar after work the next day and was more than a little disappointed when Stephan was a no-show – I waited an hour, and then left to return to my room. Shrugging my shoulders, I assigned the experience of meeting Stephan to the recesses of my mind, with just a tinge of regret.

I was sitting at my desk, working late the next evening, when the phone rang. It was Stephan, asking why I had not shown up at the bar. We discovered he had arrived an hour too early at 7 p.m., and that I had arrived just after 8 p.m., when he had already departed. At that point, it was too late to meet up; he was returning to Cape Town the following day. We did make plans to stay in contact; and in the following months, there were many hours spent on the phone chatting through the evenings. Sometimes we would have virtual lunch dates as we were getting to know each other.

In November, a long weekend loomed in Mozambique. Sandra, who was a native of Madagascar, and a member of our national staff, proposed that we take a bus from Maputo to Johannesburg for the weekend; she knew of a really nice hotel there. I thought it would be a great idea to contact Stephan to try and meet up; it had been months since we had met on Bazaruto, and the long-distance thing was going nowhere.

We arranged to meet at a popular restaurant, and Stephan drove up from Cape Town for lunch, but he needed to return home that day because he had business commitments. There is nothing like a face-toface meeting, and we had terrific fun over lunch getting to know each other a little better. It was a perfectly good lunch in an upscale café, but we decided that we would have a first proper date elsewhere.

We extravagantly decided that our next date would be a holiday together in Greece, without the interference of daily living or work obligations. I flew to Johannesburg in November and we met up at Tambo International Airport, checking in together for our adventure. There was great fun on the flight, as a couple of passengers sitting behind us had purchased a bottle of whiskey and shared it around with their fellow travelers. That got us all into a holiday mood.

We had not booked a hotel, but instead took a ferry that dropped us off at Hydra. Hydra is an island with the classic Greek white buildings with blue-tiled roofs and cobblestone streets – and there are no cars there. It was a perfect vacation spot – we swam in the Mediterranean, ate some excellent

Greek food, tried ouzo and local wines, and spent the evenings listening to live music in the local square.

After our idyllic week, I returned to Mozambique and Stephan to South Africa – both of us to our respective jobs. Later, on occasion, we would meet up in Johannesburg – and while he was great fun and we got along really well, I was cognizant that long-distance relationships were difficult to maintain. I realized that the chances of the relationship working out were very slim indeed.

The dawning of the 1990s was the beginning of radical – but badly needed – positive change in South Africa. The country's president, F.W. de Klerk, began preparing the country's first free elections with the release of anti-apartheid activist Nelson Mandela on February 11, 1990, after 33 years of imprisonment. Mandela's release was followed by the dismantling of the apartheid system in 1991. De Klerk's government then recognized and engaged with the liberation movements, including the African National Congress, which was previously considered a terrorist organization.

In September 1993, the South African legislature approved setting up a multiparty Transitional Executive Council to manage the transition to democracy; and by February 2, 1994, President de Klerk announced the most anticipated elections on the planet for April that year. Almost every black South African eligible to vote had registered to do so. Television stations from all over the globe gathered to witness the monumental, historic event. Under the leadership of Michael Manley, the former prime minister of Jamaica, a 60-member Commonwealth Observer Group arrived, along with observers from various human rights and civil society organizations to oversee the elections.

A group of 12 United Nations staff members with election experience was tasked to assist with the management of the high-level observers present.

We were in charge of the logistics – tasked to arrange the observers' accommodations, coordinate their transport, and provide translators where necessary. Our main role was to ensure that they had all the support needed to make sure that the elections would go smoothly.

South Africa was – and continues to be – a violent country; hundreds of years of suppression of the black majority by a tiny white minority naturally caused resentment, frustration and anger. On the converse side, the white minority feared that the colored and black populations would take revenge and drive them from their homes. The situation led to tension – violent outbursts were expected, which led to the presence of anti-personnel riot vehicles on the streets of Johannesburg. They were equipped with heavy armor and featured gun ports and arms for personnel to engage in crowd control.

As the support team traveled to various locations, I felt very fortunate to witness the excitement and enthusiasm within the local communities for the historic election. The UN electoral staff team worked tirelessly, operating phones and fax machines, relaying news from the townships, and stepping in where assistance was required.

When we arrived in Johannesburg, we were booked into a large hotel that was mainly taken over by UN staff working on the elections; it was situated close to the country offices. There were some days when it was a 9-to-5 job. But it was 9-to-5 with a difference – I would get to the office at 9 a.m. and would find myself leaving at 5 the following morning. On the first day that I left the office in the wee hours, there was a palpable tension as the sun began to break through the darkness.

I walked next to the huge anti-personnel vehicles with their enormous 10-foot wheels; my gut instinct kicked in, and I felt fearful. There was a distinct smell of burning in the air as I hurried along to get myself back to my hotel in one piece. I heard a thud, but it did not strike me as anything

I should be concerned about. However, a colleague who was staying on the other side of the building shouted out to me that a bomb had exploded in the middle of the street.

It left a massive crater and a trail of terror. Many people died as a result of the bomb, and the street was awash with blood and dismembered body parts. This violent incident reinforced the reality that we were working in a highly treacherous environment. Tactics such as these were designed to put the fear of God into voters – a warning to stay away from the polling stations on election day. After the incident, the United Nations office quickly relocated us to an adjacent hotel – in an equally dangerous spot.

As I was chatting with the receptionists in the new hotel, they told me that there was a murder the previous evening in a house around the corner, and that the perpetrator had burned the house down to the ground. This new hotel felt even less safe to me, considering the highly volatile environment. There were no security checks carried out on people entering the lobby, which would be considered obligatory in many African countries. There were crowds of people gathered, and as I searched the faces, I could not see any of the UN staff or election observers. Having picked up my room key, I headed for the elevator; but while waiting for it to arrive, two shady-looking men approached me from opposite directions. Instinctively, I sensed something was amiss. I stepped out of the elevator just as the doors were closing, allowing the men to ride the elevator without me and most likely saving me from a very unsavory experience.

Nevertheless, as the days merged into each other it became increasingly evident that we were witnessing history in the making. One could sense the paradigm shift; expectations were high, offering hope for millions around the world that justice would be served for South Africans who had borne the brunt of the effect of the apartheid regime.

As election day finally arrived, billions of people across the globe tuned in to the news to watch this very emotional occasion. Black South Africans were able to vote in their own country for the very first time. Long queues formed, with 18-year-olds to 98-year-olds, all grasping their voting cards and identification, and standing patiently along streets in cities and villages across the country. As the results were announced and Nelson Mandela was elected as the first black president, South Africans celebrated. I felt very privileged and grateful to be part of such a momentous occasion. It reinforced my belief in the power of democracy, and a people's right to choose their leaders.

While I was working on the elections in South Africa, I was in contact with Stephan when I had any spare moments in my day. I invited him to come up to Jo'burg, hoping for some light relief from the day-to-day pressure of the job. But he declined to make the journey, so I buried myself further in work. A little later, my birthday was approaching, and I hoped he would make an effort to come and celebrate with me; but again, he declined, saying he had other priorities. I was upset, disappointed, and more than a little angry to be left alone on my birthday. I suspected that Stephan had a girlfriend in Cape Town, or that he had simply lost interest.

Once the elections ended, I returned to Maputo and to my apartment, where I always felt safe and happy. The city brought me endless joy – I loved exploring its beautiful architecture, enjoying its great restaurants, and feeling surprised on so many occasions simply when I turned a corner to see the stunning views of the city and the shores of the Indian Ocean.

It was 1994, and Dana was finishing her senior year of high school in Indianapolis. I thought it would be a good opportunity for her to visit me in Maputo and experience a very different life. I also thought she might enjoy learning about the nature of the work I was doing in the United Nations.

She came for a couple of months, staying in the apartment; and I took some vacation leave from work. I used long weekends to take trips to South Africa and to some of the islands off the coast of Mozambique. By that time, Dana was a beautiful, confident young woman who could hold her own and had no fears about expressing her opinions. She was warm and funny, and my friends on the mission greeted her enthusiastically. It was heartwarming to see Dana enjoying her stay and embracing new experiences. It was a period of bonding for mother and daughter, creating memories that we could treasure in the years to come.

We spent a lot of time around Mozambique and Maputo, hanging out with friends and colleagues. As the sun went down one Friday evening at the end of a busy week, an invitation to a birthday party arrived from one of our security professionals. Her commitment to downtime and throwing a party knew no bounds; she was staging her own birthday party, even though she was battling malaria. I thought it would be an opportunity for a fun evening, and my request to bring Dana along was met with approval.

We put on our glad rags before heading out to the party. When we arrived, the host was draped over a chaise lounge on the veranda, wearing a beautiful kaftan and looking like some type of Cleopatra holding court with adoring fans surrounding her. Everyone sympathized with her because she was ill with malaria and could only watch her own party from the sofa.

Our attention was diverted by the presence of United Nations Deputy Special Representative of the Secretary-General Behrooz Sadry, who had taken up his position in the mission. The DSRSG was surrounded by colleagues from across the organization, and I approached him to reintroduce myself, reminding him of our previous meeting. I was dressed in black jeans and a slinky black top with a pair of comfortable Mary Jane shoes. The DSRSG's eyes were drawn down to my feet, and with a smirk on his face, he commented that my shoes were ugly. I was more than a bit surprised – I defended my fine Italian leather shoes, insisting they were beautiful. Our playful banter continued for a few minutes, drawing laughter from those who surrounded us, and I eventually excused myself and looked for a seat away from the spotlight.

Aside from the mildly amusing encounter, the rest of the party was very enjoyable as the partygoers enjoyed a respite from their work environment. I watched Dana charm my colleagues with her engaging personality, not to mention that her good looks turned the heads of some of my male colleagues. I sat on a floor cushion, taking in my surroundings, just people-watching – when the DSRSG moved away from his spot and gingerly approached me.

His reputation as a diplomat did not disappoint; he exhibited impeccable manners and requested permission to sit next to me. I responded with a smile and he pulled another floor cushion over and sat down. As we talked, I was struck by his sense of humor, intelligence, and gracious elegance, realizing how his diplomatic skills had brought him to the highest levels in the United Nations.

After some time, I excused myself to look for Dana. I discovered that she was keeping her distance on purpose. She pointed out that the DSRSG's security detail was strategically positioned around him, and had been preventing people from interrupting our conversation. I introduced Dana to him, and the DSRSG (who asked me to call him Beh) proposed that we continue the evening elsewhere. He also arranged for a driver to take Dana back to the apartment.

There were around 12 of us who continued the party across Maputo, from nightclubs to late-night bars. We continued through the night, and the sun was well up in the sky when we headed to a colleague's residence. Her home help cooked up the most delicious, much-needed breakfast before we all went back to our respective homes. As I prepared to leave, Beh asked me if I would go out with him the following evening, and on several subsequent evenings. I was flattered – and without hesitation, I accepted his invitation.

Dana stayed for a few more days before she left for South Africa to explore the possibility of working with a modeling agency. She made a bold decision to defer college for at least a year, believing that the experience and perspective gained from traveling would better prepare her for the future. After more than a month immersed in the vibrant cultures of Mozambique and South Africa, Dana returned to live with her dad. It was a time of reflection and planning as she contemplated her next steps, drawing on the rich experiences she had gathered during her time abroad.

The following week, I had prearranged a visit with Stephan to discuss the future of our relationship. Stephan was great fun and we had some wonderful times; but the geographical distance and challenges of living in two different countries cast a shadow over any possibility of taking it further. I also felt that Stephan had missed the boat by his no-show on my birthday, and that in the long term, he wasn't what I was looking for in a partner.

I told him about Beh and explained that I had met this man at a UN party, and while it was still early, I was strongly considering exploring the possibility of a new relationship. Stephan did not hide his disappointment, but I think he also understood that it was easier that way. We talked it all through and listened to each other, coming to the same conclusion in the end. There was no bickering or bitterness – we parted as friends on amicable terms, with a mutual understanding that sometimes circumstances and the paths of our lives can turn in separate directions. Yet, our respect for each other remained intact.

By the time I met Beh, he had separated from his wife, who also had worked in the UN for a brief time. She was living in New Jersey, rearing their two daughters. Our relationship did not begin straight away; it was several weeks before we really hooked up and became an item. He was an absolute gentleman, always considerate of my needs and very attentive. He wanted me at his side, attending formal receptions, elegant dinners, and prestigious gatherings. As a result, I was introduced to diplomats, dignitaries, and heads of state, and I felt a part of something extraordinary. He swept me off my feet with his charm and ability to read a situation, bringing people together and creating the most memorable experiences.

Attending a reception with Beh, Maputo, Mozambique

It seemed as though I had landed in the middle of a world beyond my wildest dreams – and it was completely unexpected. The more time we spent together, the more I became drawn to his intellect, wit, and compassion. One moment, he would engage in serious discussions about global affairs, and in the next, he would crack a joke that had everyone around him in stitches of laughter. His charisma and magnetic energy naturally drew people to him. He was very passionate about his role at the United Nations, and believed in the power of diplomacy to bridge divides and bring about positive change. Hearing him speak about his mission with such conviction made me admire him even more.

When ONUMOZ began operations in Mozambique, a peace accord had been mutually agreed upon between the rebels and the government, so the mission was charged to perform specific functions in relation to the ceasefire: to conduct elections, and to deliver humanitarian assistance to the many displaced people who relied on relief supplies.

As the end of 1994 approached, arms were handed back to military observers and decommissioned, and free and fair elections were successfully conducted. Humanitarian assistance was delivered to millions, and the country was moving into a development phase. Mozambique was much more secure; and there were clear signs from UN headquarters that the peacekeeping mission was winding down. The mission's success in restoring peace and stability to the once war-torn country was evident, thanks in no small part to Beh's exceptional negotiating skills.

While the news of Mozambique's gradual progress to peace was great news for the population, for those of us who worked during those two years, the end of the mission was viewed with a tinge of sadness. We had all come to respect and cherish those we had met along the way; the locals who worked alongside us to maintain peace had shown amazing resilience. I was also going to miss Mozambique's stunning coastline, fabulous seafood, and the charming piano bar in the Polana Serena Hotel that had been a backdrop to many fun and entertaining evenings.

As the countdown began and the time to leave Mozambique neared, it was time to bid farewell to friends and colleagues. I found myself discussing the inevitable return to work in New York. Many of my colleagues felt the need for a complete break from the hustle and bustle of mission life and headed off to exotic destinations, like the Seychelles and Mauritius.

I knew that Beh was missing the vibrancy of the familiar streets in New York, the city that never sleeps. I was, however, looking for one last adventure in Africa before returning to the concrete jungle. I decided since I had not yet made it quite as far as Cape Town, I would take a few days to explore the jewel of South Africa.

Stephan had spoken about the symbolism of Table Mountain – its cultural and historical significance for the local communities. The people see it as a spiritual place and representative of their heritage; its slopes bear traces of evidence of early human habitation. The sophisticated Victoria and Alfred Waterfront, situated along the harbor on the Atlantic, boasts some of the finest restaurants in the city, and serves some particularly decent local wines.

In Mozambique, there were lots of farewell parties, as former colleagues who had become good friends prepared for departure. I bid my friends farewell and headed off; but before I did, I contacted Stephan to see if he could help me secure a hotel in Cape Town where I would feel safe. I also asked him to recommend some places to visit. Being the gentleman that he was, he offered to pick me up from the airport and deliver me to the hotel. He also appeared the next day and we had a wonderful time visiting the sights and fabulous vineyards, and dining in some fine establishments. Stephan even brought me to his parents' store and introduced me to his charming family.

I had told Beh of my previous relationship with Stephan, and because we were now just friends, I purposely had not told Beh that I had recently made contact with Stephan. After just a few days in Cape Town I was starting to really miss Beh, so I called him on his personal landline in the office, and he picked up. As the conversation progressed, he asked what I was up to. I felt I had nothing to hide, so I told him that Stephan was showing me the sights of the city. The unexpected news caught him off guard and he was quite angry with me. I was later told by a colleague that he was so annoyed with me that he played cards incessantly for the next three days, so he could focus on something else except yours truly.

Returning to
New York

I did not hear from Beh when I returned to New York, and I did not
contact him. I was back in my former position at UNFPA, and after
several weeks I became comforted by the familiarity and normality of
life in New York.

One day, I was meeting a friend for a drink in the Delegates Lounge
in the United Nations Building to catch up on the news and gossip that I
missed during my sojourn in Mozambique. I rose to leave the lounge, heading for home, when I ran into Beh – who was just entering. In such a huge
building with thousands of staff, it was a chance encounter, and it felt like
the universe was conspiring to bring us together.

We picked up the relationship where we left off, without missing a beat; it was as if we had never parted. We started to meet on a regular basis, going to dinners, theater, drinks – just enjoying each other's company. Beh's charisma and charm were undeniable. Witnessing the genuine affection and respect that everyone held for him was heartwarming. Whenever we gathered at the United Nations Delegates Lounge on Friday evenings, he would be greeted with warm embraces from his colleagues. It was a testament to the lasting impact he had on those around him.

Evening drinks with Beh at United Nations Delegates Lounge

As the months passed, our bond deepened, and our friendship-turned-courtship blossomed into something more profound. He was not just a charming companion; he had become a dear confidant and a source of unwavering support. We shared our hopes, dreams, and fears, finding repose in each other's empathy. There were great differences, but also so many similarities, between our childhoods. The more time we spent together, delving into the makeup of our lives – particularly our shared experiences from our challenging childhoods – an unbreakable bond began to form between us.

Beh was born in Tehran, before Persia became known as Iran. He came from an influential family, where his uncle was a judge and his father a member of the senate. However, he too lost his mom as a young boy when his parents divorced. In Islamic tradition, the children stay with the father after a divorce; so, while I grew up spending time with my maternal grandmother, he was sent to live with his paternal grandmother. Subsequently, at the age of 10, he was packed off to boarding school in Paris, France.

Not only did Beh excel academically, speaking flawless Farsi, French and English, he was also an excellent sportsman and a fairly decent soccer player (according to himself). He was 21 when he traveled to visit his father's brother in New York, seeking advice. Beh had contemplated a career in dentistry, but the visit was a game changer. After many hours in conversation, his favored uncle suggested that Beh try a career in the United Nations rather than a career looking into patients' mouths.

And so he passed his exams with flying colors, and began working in the UN in a somewhat lowly role in the library. However, his innate talents in diplomacy and language skills saw him climb rapidly through the ranks. He became a career diplomat and negotiator, rising to the rank of assistant secretary-general.

We both came from countries where poverty was endemic and people were repressed. My childhood experiences were rooted in the cruelty of the communist ideology; Beh's childhood was spent mainly alone in Paris for nearly a decade. His family members who remained in Iran were governed by the autocratic rule of the shah of Iran. Ultimately, the shah was deposed during a revolution in 1979, when a more autocratic (and theocratic) ruler, the Ayatollah Khomeini, came to power and led the rebel group.

When we were together, we would spend hours upon hours talking, often until the sun peeped over the horizon. We were sharing stories, unearthing memories, and finding the similarities and commonalities in our life experiences. Although we were lovers by that time, it was during our conversations that he began calling me his "best friend." That was unexpected, and it carried a lot of weight. There were times when I struggled to understand the depth of what that meant to him, but I knew that I held a special place in his heart.

I could not deny the overwhelming connection that enveloped us. Time with him felt like I had found my way home – a sanctuary of calm in my sometimes chaotic life. I found myself sharing everything with Beh and becoming more confident in our relationship. Each day spent together felt brighter, the air lighter, with a growing happiness. I felt special; I felt loved and cherished. In the late 1990s, several years after we met, Beh and I moved in together in New York – to share a home and a life. At that point, we were inseparable.

The breakdown of communist Europe had begun in late 1989 with the fall of the Berlin Wall, which had been erected 38 years prior. It was the beginning of the end of communism, and European countries were shaking off the shackles of a dark age. War was also looming again in Europe, with the breakup of Yugoslavia. While Yugoslavia had adopted a more decentralized and less repressive form of government compared with other eastern European communist states, the breakup there was due to cultural and religious divisions between the ethnic groups. The memories of atrocities committed by all sides during World War II was an added factor.

Beh's name was put forward as the United Nations assistant secretary-general (ASG) to be located in Zagreb, Croatia, where fierce fighting was then taking place. Slovenia had overwhelmingly voted for independence in December 1990, and in May 1991, a referendum in Croatia also supported full independence from the former Yugoslavia. Slovenia and Croatia both proclaimed formal independence on June 25, 1991. However, when the Serb minority in Croatia declared its own independence from the Croatian republic and expressed its desire to join Serbia, violent conflict broke out. The Yugoslav army intervened in the conflict to separate combatants, but it became quickly apparent that the army favored the Croatian Serbs. The war that followed devastated Croatia, resulting in tens of thousands dead, and hundreds of thousands of people displaced[1].

I had no inkling that Beh had been offered the assistant-secretary-general post, so it came as a huge surprise when he announced his new mission when we went out to dinner one Friday evening. Before I had a chance to get upset because we would be separated by distance and time, he announced that his greatest wish would be for me to join him on the mission with the UN Protection Force (UNPROFOR), to be based in Zagreb. Without so much as one second of hesitation, I responded with a resounding "yes."

The next Monday morning, I began seeking a release from my position at UNFPA. My superiors were none too pleased that once again, I was looking to head off on a mission.

As the days passed, the cogs on the wheels of the UN bureaucracy began to align and gain momentum. My sense of anticipation grew as the preparations for a deployment to Zagreb took shape. After what felt like an eternity, the day finally arrived when I received word that my release was granted. My chance of obtaining another release after two previous missions had been doubtful, so I suspect that Beh had played some part in securing my discharge.

I saw my new assignment as another wonderful opportunity to witness history, experience a different part of the world, and learn on the job. Of course Beh was to lead the mission, and I was to work in logistics, so we could see and be with each other every day. With an adrenaline rush kicking in, I could not contain my excitement and relief. It was difficult to hide just how happy I felt as I packed my bags. I was ready to start another new chapter in my life as I boarded the flight to Zagreb to join Beh at our new mission.

Croatia

It was September 1995 when I arrived in Croatia and settled into my role. I was assigned to a unit handling United Nations property and contingent-owned equipment. It was another new role, and I put my head down to learn the duties I was expected to perform. The conflict was escalating, with random violent outbursts occurring across the country. It was difficult not to shake the feeling that time was of the essence. My colleagues were acutely aware of the urgency to increase efforts to bring peace and stability to those whose lives were in danger and to the communities that were displaced.

The purpose of the mission was to protect civilians, but the presence of an intergovernmental alliance force added another layer of complexity. Members of the intergovernmental force occupied buildings just a block away from the UN building and they served as a stark reminder of the gravity of the situation. It added another dimension to the collaborative efforts of the UN.

As with previous missions, friendships formed with the most unusual and interesting people – people you would never have the opportunity to meet in a regular job. One such person was Major Hogan, a major with the British Royal Armed Forces. A liaison between the UN and the peacekeeping force, Major Hogan was a handsome young man with a twinkle in his eye. He was always in good form and had an ability to lighten the mood, even on the darkest of days during the conflict. He was frequently in and out of the office where I worked, and would stop by for a few words or to share a joke.

Major Hogan went so far as to "procure" me a military ID after I complained that I did not have access to the Officers' Mess. He marched me across the road over to the military office, and introduced me to two officers as a new recruit – a Polish captain about to be invested into the mission. The officers had no idea that it was one of Major Hogan's jokes, and I was questioned about my experience and my role in the Polish army. Playing the role with my best broken Polish accent, the first thing that came to my mind – and out of my mouth – was that I was a gunner in my home country. The two officers did not bat an eyelid as they took my photo and handed me the prestigious ID, which to this day remains one of my most treasured mementos of my time in Croatia.

The ID was not the only "friends' benefit" that Hogan provided. Although we worked every day of the week, there were occasions when we would be allocated some in-country rest and recreation (R&R), mainly to ensure we didn't suffer from burnout, an all too frequent consequence of overwork and stress on missions.

The military had organized a barbecue behind the Zagreb airport, with some fun games to entertain the non-military personnel. They even offered a lesson in driving an army tank for anyone who was interested. Not being one to let such an opportunity pass, I put myself forward for the special driving lesson. The tank was parked outside the barbecue area; an officer escorted me to the combat vehicle, which weighed more than 50 tons. I climbed into the turret to take charge of the massive beast. The officer guided me through navigating the gears and I learned that these machines can reach speeds of 30 to 40 miles per hour. Of course, unlike a car on wheels, a tank moves along on tracks. I managed to negotiate hills and roads for the next 20 minutes or so. Thankfully, I was never called on to ever drive a tank again; even so, I had Major Hogan to thank for the biggest adrenaline rush imaginable.

We frequently had to use helicopters in conflict zones to get from point A to B. Travel by road can be slow and very dangerous in such a situation, and can give combatants an opportunity to attack the vehicles. There was also the reality of increased risk from unexploded ordnance devices – in other words, land mines – that had been planted to maximize damage to the unfortunate person who unwittingly set them off.

Arriving in Sarajevo

The United Nations heavily invests in a Department of Safety and Security to protect its staff and minimize loss of life during missions. Sadly, there were still many staff members who lost their lives in service over the years.

I was assigned to assist the head of peacekeeping at a high-level meeting as part of a contingent from UN headquarters in Sarajevo. My role was as a notetaker, to ensure that there were accurate and precise details of such meetings.

We headed out to the military airfield, which was cordoned off from the main public airport in Zagreb, and boarded the military helicopter. Once strapped into our seats, and before we were given earplugs and headphones to dim the noise of the rotors, we received our safety instructions from the co-pilot. As the engine was engaged, the blades began to slowly turn, picking up speed for about three minutes before we lifted off.

A second helicopter flew next to us for safety. The sliding door of the helicopter remained open, where two soldiers were seated. They wore seat belts to hold themselves in, as they leaned forward to observe what was happening on the ground. They each had a rather large machine gun between their legs, in the event that some random rebel decided to take a potshot at our flight. In such situations, flares are set off automatically from the helicopter to trick any heat-seeking missile into hitting the burning flare, rather than the target. The helicopter ride to Sarajevo was thrilling and at the same time nerve-racking, and can only be described as a natural shot of adrenaline. I had never experienced anything like that before, and it certainly made me feel fully alive.

As the weeks passed, the UN mission was refined, and procedures were put in place to better deliver on humanitarian and development needs. Staff worked from morning till night, and Beh was ever ready to show his appreciation for his team.

Aware of the need for time out from the job and with an opportunity to decompress and enjoy a few beers, Beh would host a happy hour on Friday evenings. Sometimes we would head to the casino after drinks, where he would enjoy playing blackjack as I watched. It was another way he would decompress after a hard week's work.

A private moment at a reception, Zagreb, Croatia

Beh's job was done when he was able to split UNPROFOR into three separate missions with separate mandates; and so it was time for him to head back to New York. He wanted me to return with him; but UNFPA had granted me a release for 12 months. I had made a commitment and wanted to see the contract out, so I chose to remain.

After Beh left for New York, I filled my days with work, often leaving the office late in the evenings. Zagreb is beautiful, with a great public transportation system, including excellent tram lines that crisscross the city. However, the sidewalks can sometimes turn into the road without any obvious transition.

It was a Friday evening, and I was doing some shopping on my way home when I attempted to maneuver around a car that was pulling out slowly from the non-existent curb. As I walked out onto the street, I heard people around me screaming. I knew I was not screaming, so I had no idea why there were such piercing screams ringing in the air. I decided that they were screaming about what was going to happen behind me, so I decided not to turn around. With my heart pounding and my resolve steeled, I continued to move forward, determined not to let fear dictate my path. I was concerned that I might lose my footing – not knowing the danger that was behind me.

Within seconds, tons of steel hit my left shoulder and the impact threw me onto the vehicle attempting to move into the flow of traffic. I looked up to see a tram continuing on its journey. The driver had provided no warning, no signal; he knew he hit me and didn't bother to stop to see if I was dead or alive. People gathered around; and with shock visible on their faces, they watched me stand up. With the embarrassment of having all that unwanted attention, I did a quick check of myself and didn't think I had any broken bones. And, there were no visible signs of blood, so I diagnosed myself as only a little dazed. I continued my trip to pick up rental videos for the weekend, but after I got to the store I realized I couldn't move my left arm. I used my right arm to pick up a video and made it home.

Trying to remove my coat was a little painful. As I disrobed in front of the mirror, I could see some severe bruising along my left side, which had turned totally black. I think that shock kicked in; my body began to go into spasms. I was in a foreign country, without the ability to speak the language, and had no idea what to do or how to explain what had happened.

The phone rang, and it was Beh, asking if everything was OK. It was as if he had sensed there was something wrong. When I told him that I had been hit by a tram, he assumed I had been in a car and began questioning me as to who was driving. I had to explain that I had not been in a car, but was walking on my way home. Before we finished our conversation, Beh had booked himself on a flight to Zagreb.

I spent the weekend going from my bed to the kitchen, swallowing every cold medication and aspirin in the cupboards I could find to relieve the muscle spasms and severe pain. It never occurred to me to call someone from the office for help.

On Monday morning, I arrived back at work and told my colleagues what had happened three days previously. Without hesitation, my boss called for a UN driver to take me to the hospital for an X-ray. I was escorted by a local person so he could explain to the doctors what had happened. It turned out that I had several broken ribs, along with a very badly bruised arm, and I was ordered to go on sick leave until I was fit enough to return to work.

Beh arrived the following day, and the sight of him arriving on my doorstep was worth a dozen painkillers – he lifted my mood so much. He set about making everything comfortable for me. Anticipating my difficulties in washing, dressing, and trying to cook, he took care of my every need over the next two weeks while I recovered with my ribs bandaged.

War was still raging through the eastern flanks of Croatia as the main mission was disbanded. Staff were either returning to headquarters or being redeployed to one of the three new missions. I opted to join the UN Transitional Authority in Eastern Slavonia (UNTAES), operating out of Vukovar, Croatia. Vukovar, some 300 kilometers from Zagreb, is located in the northeast part of the country, where the Danube River provides a natural border between the city and Serbia. It was the site of one of the fiercest battles during the 1991 war, and was the city that saw the most destruction than any other city during the wars in Croatia and Bosnia.

Over the centuries, Vukovar had been part of Hungary; the Ottoman Empire; the Austrian Habsburg monarchy; the Kingdom of Serbs, Croats, and Slovenes; Yugoslavia; and eventually independent Croatia. It had historically been a prosperous town in the rich agricultural eastern Slavonia region. There were around 44,000 inhabitants in the city in the 1991 census, where 37.4 percent identified as Serbs, and more than 43.7 per cent as Croats.[2] An 87-day siege took place there; Vukovar was captured by the Yugoslav Army. Around 80,000 died during the conflict, and Vukovar had been razed to the ground, so much so that it resembled a demolition site. Vukovar was the first place in Europe to be so heavily damaged since WWII. [3] Vukovar would not come under Croatian rule until January 1998, when UNTAES concluded its mission.

Eastern Slavonia

I managed to hitch a ride on the UN shuttle to Vukovar, uncertain about my post. When I arrived at our new headquarters, I found my name on the door with the title "Board of Inquiry" beneath it. I had previously sat on two UN boards; but this time, I was the person in charge of setting up the systems for the inquiry.

I hadn't brought any rules or regulations for the position with me – all the documentation was back in Zagreb. So once again, I hitched a ride, back to Zagreb, and returned with as much information as I could find to set up the systems necessary for the board to become operational.

Once renowned for its baroque architecture when it was ruled by the Habsburgs, there was nothing left of Vukovar except piles of rubble. Not a single building survived intact. Residents collected pieces of furniture found among the ruins, and broke them up to use as firewood. The glow of fires could be seen across the city in the evening, as people sat huddled around for warmth. The fires also doubled as a way for people to cook meager rations in an effort to keep families from starvation. There were just a handful of buildings that were habitable, so families slept outdoors or in makeshift tents, trying to keep close together to share body heat. Some of our local staff had family members who were living in such conditions; and indeed, some had watched their family members die during the shelling on their homes. On one particular day on my way into the UN offices, I was horrified to see a body floating down the Danube River. For me, the heartbreaking stories from our own staff drove me to work even harder to facilitate the work of the peace negotiators.

Finding accommodations as a foreigner was difficult in the midst of conflict, but I was lucky to find a room to share with some female UN colleagues. We shared bedrooms in a small apartment, where one of the rugs had rather large red stains. I could only imagine that some unfortunate person had been killed there and that the red stain was that person's blood.

Vukovar, Eastern Slavonia

There was a dining hall in the UN building where we could eat breakfast and lunch. A Purchase Exchange (PX) store was opened on the grounds of our headquarters, and we could buy things like food and cooking gas, which allowed us to cook the fresh vegetables – when or if we could find them – and frozen meats bought in the PX. While Zagreb had some level of normalcy, nothing remained in Vukovar – no access to stores or places like video shops. There was zero entertainment to help us wind down after a stressful work day. This made each day the same as the one before – it was a constant repetition of eat, work and bed.

My own work organizing the Board of Inquiry was demanding, and it kept me busy setting up the office and ensuring that the necessary protocols were in place. Then, a few months after I landed in Vukovar, I managed to find a newly renovated house and moved in with two roommates. The house allowed each of us to have a bedroom, which was a huge luxury. However, on a day-to-day basis, there were challenges with intermittent electricity, and the freezing winter temperatures were particularly difficult. Many days, it was easier to just keep working – the UN offices had generators and access to heat.

I was very grateful to exist in such a privileged position in Vukovar, as I watched the townspeople struggle each day for basic survival. They had witnessed death and destruction; but their resilience was inspirational, and they coped in the most brutal conditions without complaint. In such moments, I remembered my grandmother's wisdom; she taught me that in life, all we can do is carry on with our work, giving our best each day to survive and persevere.

Beh was 19 years older than me; so, not long after he returned to New York, he retired. Beh had served in the UN for more than 40 years, working in the world of diplomacy where his skills were utilized to move several peace accords forward across a war-torn world. He was my constant companion, and his support was such a comfort during difficult times. Beh's first trip after retirement was to fly over to visit me in Vukovar, and he ended up staying on, moving into the house. His presence made my life easier and I loved having him by my side – someone to come home to in the evenings and who understood the daily challenges of my work life.

Beh stayed on with me until heightened tensions in northern Angola boiled over again in 1996. This time, the conflict there was around oil resources, and there was a resurgence of violence. Consequently, like many retired senior diplomats of quality in the United Nations, Beh was asked to come out of retirement. He was just a few months retired when the UN offered him a position as DSRSG back in Angola; and so, in March 1996, we left Vukovar, and together we returned to Luanda.

Angola

It felt strange to return to Angola after four years to work in Luanda in a totally different context. I was now living with Beh in the capital city, rather than working in a remote post in a regional office. We had a house in a secure compound, with protection officers around the clock. As Beh took on the responsibilities of deputy for the mission, I found myself working in the Board of Inquiry office once again, but this time as a member of the board. My previous experience elevated me from an administrative position to a permanent member of the board – investigating deaths, serious injury cases and traffic accidents.

Luanda was quite different from Maputo in terms of its architecture and climate – the heat had been sweltering in Maputo, with no breeze coming in off the ocean to cool us down. The sun beat down relentlessly there, making some days feel as if we were living in an inferno. The heat was so extreme that there were times when I felt like someone was putting needles into my skin and my eyeballs were burning.

Going to a official reception in Luanda

There were many weekends when Beh was busy working and I was not required in the office. Having some downtime, I decided to take in some rays and focus on working on my tan. After a few hours lying in the sun,

I went to stand up to get a bottle of water from the fridge when I keeled over, collapsing beside my sunchair. Totally disoriented, I found myself on my hands and knees, crawling to the sink to fetch some water. Only then did I realize the seriousness of the situation – I was severely dehydrated and dangerously close to passing out. Mild dehydrations can play havoc with blood pressure, heart rate and body temperature while severe dehydration can lead to kidney failure, brain damage and even death. With a bottle of water in hand, I sipped slowly, feeling immense relief as the H2O provided the necessary solution for my parched body.

As for Beh, he was on call 24/7, frequently excusing himself from the table at dinners. Sometimes, because of the six hour time difference with New York, he would get out of bed in the middle of the night to take crucial calls. He worked tirelessly with total dedication to the mission.

When Beh had to travel outside the compound, often to high-level government meetings, or functions at various embassies, he was accompanied by personal protection and traveled in a convoy for safety so they could speed through the city. Such precautions reduced the chances of a random rebel attack.

Traveling outside the compound could be dangerous, and I felt uncomfortable in some situations. But of course it was part of my job, and despite any fear I was feeling at the time, I had to put my head down and get on with it. In UN missions where there is ongoing conflict, the consequence of living in such unpredictability can result in extreme stress. The reality is that the UN is frequently a target of disgruntled armed rebels, and there have been many attacks on UN compounds over the years. In such insecure and volatile situations, R&R (rest and relaxation) can be allocated on a four-week rotation to prevent burnout and allow time for staff members to de-stress. The mission's R&R destination was nearby South Africa; our go-to break was Cape Town. We escaped there every couple of months, taking time to relax – and also taking time to try out some of the excellent wines in the vineyards around the city.

In the summer of 1997, Beh was becoming increasingly frustrated with incidents at work. As a true professional, he never shared the details of any disputes or differences he encountered, but it was obvious that he was unimpressed by – and quite angry at – some developments taking place at a very high level. It came as no surprise, then, when news arrived that we would be leaving the mission and returning to New York. Beh's mood lightened with this decision, but the reasons behind it remained a mystery to me as we began the process of packing and preparing to depart.

Back in New York in June 1997, we settled into the familiar rhythm of the city. I returned to work as Beh made the most of city life. He would head out for morning coffee with his newspaper under his arm, frequently meeting up with other retired colleagues.

By that time, Dana was 23, and she would travel to New York so we could spend time together. She had quit college and moved to Chicago, where she and her boyfriend, Chris, were planning their life together. We kept in constant touch, and I would either visit her in Chicago or she would come visit me in New York. We enjoyed our time together, doing mother-daughter things. I hadn't met her beau, but she related how she and Chris had met and fell in love. I was happy that she had such high hopes for a bright future with this young man.

One Friday evening in our apartment, Beh and I were settling in and finishing cleanup after dinner. We switched on the TV to see what was happening in the world, and a news flash appeared on our screen that left us in a state of shock. Beh's boss in Angola, SRSG Alioune Blondin Beye, was one of five members of the UN Observer Mission in Angola who were involved in a plane crash. The plane went down as it was approaching the Ivory Coast capital of Abidjan. All passengers and the crew who were traveling on mission died in the crash. Eyewitnesses reported that the plane was on fire before it crash-landed, lending credence to the Angolan prime minister's statement that he believed the accident happened under unusual circumstances. We knew everyone who had died in that crash; and most likely Beh would have been on that flight had he still been working. It was a sobering realization, and I was grateful he had made the decision to leave the mission.

* * *

For the next three years, I was back with UNFPA, resuming my role in the population fund and working in an administrative position with the Asia division. It was quite the change from running a Board of Inquiry in a war zone, but I appreciated that I was privileged to have so many missions under my belt. And regardless of my rank, I worked every bit as hard as if I was back on mission.

The work was certainly not stressful; it came with minimal responsibility, and it certainly did not tax my brain. There were many disgruntled colleagues when I returned, and I found that the most mundane tasks were being dumped on me. I was drowning in mountains of paperwork, which I worked my way through. Still, I considered myself lucky. There was no point in complaining – I was very grateful that there was a job waiting for me each time I returned from a mission.

The return to New York also gave me some routine, security and surety. It allowed me to recover from some of the shocking sights and uncertainty I experienced when I was living on the edge. Beh enjoyed his well-earned retirement, as well as the simple joys of home life. He often had my dinner on the table when I returned home, and nothing gave him more joy than fussing over me, attending to my needs.

Our weekends were spent hosting dinner parties and visiting friends and former colleagues. We were regular attendees at Broadway plays and shows, savored leisurely strolls through Central Park, and generally enjoyed all that the Big Apple has to offer.

The more time we spent together, the easier and more comfortable we became with each other. We would almost finish each other's sentences. We shared the same sense of humor, and the same taste in food and furnishings. We could communicate silently, instinctively knowing what the other was looking for. We could read each other's mood. As one year rolled into the next, Beh's presence was responsible for my increased confidence. I began to radiate a peaceful and calm aura. Living with Beh became a source of deep reassurance; his gentle acts of kindness brought me such comfort.

I was very moved when the 2000 census form arrived in our mailbox and Beh took it upon himself to complete it for us. In that simple act, I was secure in the knowledge that he would always be my steadfast companion. He was what had been missing in my earlier life: a friend, a confidant, a man who showed me kindness. I had met so few like him in my years on this earth.

As my own love life flourished, Dana arrived for dinner one summer's day. She introduced us to Christopher (Chris), who I found to be a lovely young man with impeccable manners. They had been dating for a year or more before we had the opportunity to meet this man who had captured my daughter's heart. Dana and her beau were spending a weekend in New York, so we had plenty of opportunity to size him up, and I was more than happy when they announced their engagement on New Year's Eve of 2000. They were looking forward to a new millennium of hope and positivity, with plans for a summer wedding in 2001.

Wedding preparations went into overdrive: Dana's dress, the bridesmaid dresses, the rings, the honeymoon, the reception venue, the church… it was full-on. I was eager to contribute to Dana's big day and jumped in, offering to pay for the wedding without realizing what was involved. My mistake was in thinking that it was going to be a quiet, intimate affair with close family and a few friends. I hadn't realized that Chris came from a large family, with brothers, sisters, aunts, uncles, and cousins. And, Dana and Chris had a circle of friends, all of whom wanted to be part of their big day.

As the specifics became more evident and the costs were mounting, I was trying to talk them down from spending so much on a single day. I felt I had allocated a generous budget, but when I saw a guest list adding up to several hundred people, it sent terror through me, drowning my well-intentioned offer in a sea of financial impossibility. Dana wanted the whole fairy-tale wedding, but it would have left me in debt to fund something so extravagant. I was not prepared for that.

Our conversation turned into a minefield of life's unmet expectations. I knew she had reasons for some of her grievances; our separation because of my work was not the ideal way to grow up – but it was the best I could do in the circumstances. I had hoped that she understood the sacrifices I had made, how much she was loved and wanted, and how her move to live with her dad was in her best interest. Most of my life, I worked to support Dana and provide the best I could possibly afford – supporting her wishes, her education, the purchase of her two cars (both of which were written off after accidents), and her travel to Europe and Africa.

As the tension between us became more pronounced, and communications were dialed down to zero, it led Dana to a decision that floored me. She called one morning as I was preparing to return to Africa, with the news that she and Chris had decided to postpone the wedding – to put it on hold indefinitely. The weight of Dana's decision broke my heart. As I meticulously went through the process of canceling the reservations we had painstakingly arranged for the summer nuptials, it felt like the dismantling of a dream we had built together. Each cancellation was a painful reminder of the fragility of relationships.

Then, while I was miles away in Africa, and without any communication between us, the news reached me – Dana had married in my absence. Sadness and disappointment surged through me; I felt like my heartache was reverberating across the continents. I clung to my silence, unable to bridge the divisions that had formed between us. The space that once held shared dreams, laughter, and mother-daughter camaraderie now stood barren.

By all accounts, the wedding was a small enough celebration; and in fairness to Dana and Chris, they threw in every cent they possessed to turn it into a day that was special for them. It just happened without me. Still, I never once stopped loving my beautiful daughter.

Dana had continued to confide in Joanna – they remained close, almost like sisters. She had persuaded Joanna not to tell me anything about the wedding; and she also would ask Joanna not to tell me about the birth of her children, my grandchildren. On my part, I never pushed Joanna to tell me what was going on; I was just glad that Dana had someone to confide in and trust.

As time went on, my heartache deepened with my daughter's continuing estrangement from me. The rift denied me the privilege of witnessing the early years of those precious infant grandchildren. The pain was particularly poignant because I longed to be an integral part of their lives – to hold those precious babies in my arms, and share in the wonder of their growth. The missed opportunities, the years when I was absent from their lives, are a painful source of sadness that still weighs heavily on my soul. The reality of those moments that I never had a chance to cherish continue to haunt me.

Mission Impossible

Beh's retirement allowed him to spend his mornings flicking channels to catch up on the latest news. He didn't have much of an interest in local news and would switch channels from CNN to Al Jazeera to BBC World, keeping pace with what was happening across the globe. His interest in politics and conflict never waned. On a hot summer's day in 2000, in our Manhattan apartment, we were watching the news, when the program was interrupted with a news bulletin. The Revolutionary United Front (RUF) – a rebel army in Sierra Leone – had kidnapped more than 500 hostages, holding them captive. At the time, Sierra Leone was experiencing an ongoing, brutal civil war that kicked off when diamonds were discovered in the eastern part of the country. The RUF was fighting for control of the country and was using diamonds to trade for arms, leading to the term "blood diamonds."

When the news finished, I remarked to Beh that the United Nations would surely call him to assist in the negotiations for the hostages. He laughed at the idea and proceeded to put the kettle on to make a cup of coffee; he was, at that time, a good three years into retirement. Not one hour later, the phone rang. It was the United Nations, summoning Beh to participate in negotiations to secure the release of the hostages.

The next day, after rising early and going to the back of the wardrobe to select a work suit, he left our apartment for UN headquarters. He looked every bit the well-dressed, confident diplomat who had never lost his touch. At headquarters, he was briefed on the gravity of the situation, which was a lot more serious than the news media had reported. It was a life-and-death situation for those who were captured, and Beh left for Sierra Leone on the first available flight, with a return flight booked in two weeks' time.

Despite the abysmal communications in Sierra Leone, Beh and I continued to be in contact as often as feasible, in defiance of the distance. The UN was hinting that it would greatly benefit the mission if Beh could stay on in Sierra Leone, so our conversations centered around the pros and cons of extending his stay.

The two-week mission turned into a month; a formal invitation was issued requesting Beh to stay on so the mission would benefit from his expertise. Beh, as on previous occasions, wanted me by his side and asked me to join him. I didn't hesitate, and once again set about seeking release from my post with UNFPA in New York.

Beh's influence and rank within the United Nations ensured my early release, and I arrived in Sierra Leone by helicopter via Conakry, the capital of Guinea. Sierra Leone's airport, located in Lungi, was not operational. And with the civil war in full swing, it was considered too dangerous to fly commercial airlines into the country; so, the UN used helicopters to complete the 128-kilometer journey. Once again, Beh was appointed as deputy representative of the secretary-general, to the UN mission in Sierra Leone (UNAMSIL). He immersed himself in his duties as a peace negotiator for the release of the hostages. Then, when I arrived, I was entrusted with the responsibility to set up the Board of Inquiry Secretariat, not an insignificant task.

Sierra Leone

U NAMSIL's mandate was to initiate and support the peace process during the civil war. Established in 1999, the mission's specific role was to facilitate the disarmament and demobilization of various armed factions, monitor the cease-fire, protect civilians, and assist in reestablishing state authority.

Sierra Leone (meaning "Lion Mountain") has a long history of colonization. It was part of the British Empire, as England ruled the country from 1808 to 1961. The British used Sierra Leone as a labor asset, exporting and selling slaves to the Americas and the Caribbean. While power was handed back to the people in 1961, and elections were held in 1967, there was a military coup that saw Siaka Stevens take control as prime minister (later president). It was the beginning of a dictatorship that exploited the valuable minerals discovered in the east of the country.

Feeling left out of the asset-grab of diamonds and mineral resources, former politician Foday Sankoh – who had trained in the Liberian military – formed the RUF in 1991 to challenge the status quo. What transpired was a bloody and cruel civil war that lasted for 11 years and saw countless deaths and millions displaced. The RUF committed horrendous crimes, abducting children to form its core fighting force. After kidnapping the children, they compelled the kids to take drugs and commit atrocities in their own villages – often against their own families – so that these children would feel unable to turn to anyone but the RUF for support and protection. Girls were abducted, forced to marry the rebels and used as sex slaves, and then ostracized by their communities when they were discarded for newer wives. The RUF roamed villages and towns, instilling terror among the communities. The RUF rebels were known for hacking off limbs of the villagers, using the phrase "long sleeve, short sleeve" as a question pertaining to the type of amputation the victim would prefer.

One day, I came across a woman in a wheelchair who had no arms or legs; and I was told that she once had a sandwich stall on the beach, which provided enough income for her to support and feed her family. It was common for men and women to set up sandwich stalls at markets or beaches. Or, they would just walk around local neighborhoods with large containers on their heads, selling the sandwiches. The sandwiches are made with *tapalapa* bread, a favorite among Sierra Leoneans; it has a heavy and dense inside that is reminiscent of soft pretzels, but the outside has a deliciously crispy crust.

I was told by a driver that a couple of teenage boys tried to steal from the woman with the sandwich stall one day, and she reprimanded them. But the same teenagers returned within the hour and hacked off the woman's arms and legs as "punishment" for their reprimand. It was a story that was repeated over and over again in that violent, brutal, drug-fueled conflict.

The coastal area of Freetown is lucky enough to have Lumni Beach, which looks stunningly beautiful at a distance, but up close it was covered with litter and used needles dumped from a local medical facility. Just off the beach was the Mammy Yoko Hotel, which had been the scene of a fierce battle against Nigerian forces in 1997, and where bullet hole scars were still visible in its walls when we arrived. In a country decimated by war, the hotel was the best and safest accommodation available for the mission. Bedrooms were turned into offices and the top floor was reserved for accommodations, which is where Beh and I set up our living quarters.

Sierra Leone is a tropical country with annual monsoons; so, as in every other bedroom in the hotel, the room assigned to us was dank and reeked of mold. The room's broken furniture was crudely held together with string and nails. With the prospect of living in this hotel for the foreseeable future, we were determined to make it more comfortable; and so, we took matters into our own hands.

Late one night, well past midnight and well beyond working hours, we explored the hotel to search for decent furniture to exchange with the items in our room. We searched the corridors with a torch light, hoping to find anything that could improve our living space. Finally, our efforts paid off. We stumbled upon some usable furniture that we brought back to our room. With great delight, we exchanged the old, broken furniture for undamaged pieces, making our space more livable. We shared laughs as we rummaged through the hotel to create a space to call our own. The living area we created would help insulate us from the horrors that existed outside for the many innocent civilians experiencing the brutality of a vicious conflict.

Finding food in Freetown was another challenge. With no cooking facilities in Mammy Yoko, we relied on restaurant food for the first few months. The damage left by the war left just one restaurant operational; its menu was exclusively seafood. While seafood is undoubtedly a healthy choice, consuming it daily for two months led to total monotony. The few open grocery stores scattered around Freetown were mostly located on the opposite side of town; but if you tried to travel across the city, you could become caught up in traffic that would stand still for hours on end. It was just too much work for anyone to cross the city to access grocery stores.

Beh's Lebanese friend Daher, who had survived a rebel attack and chose to remain in Sierra Leone, extended invitations to us and other UN colleagues to enjoy sumptuous Lebanese cuisine at his regular home gatherings. Lebanese food is always tasty, but Daher's feasts were exceptional – and a welcome relief from our monotonous everyday diet. Daher provided us with an abundance of flavors that left us wanting more. Thankfully, as time went on, the UN set up a small PX store at the Mammy Yoko compound, and imported European and American foodstuffs so we could enjoy some sense of normality.

Bureh Town, Sierra Leone With UN friends, Sunday

Beyond Freetown on the most southern part of the peninsula is Bureh Town, a beautiful beach with pristine white sand and crystal-clear blue water. On weekends and holidays, the coastal haven offered us a welcome refuge from the realities of the war-torn country. Also, Daher had a house on the idyllic beach there; and while it had come under rebel attack during the conflict and was utterly demolished, it still provided us with safe shelter while being rebuilt.

There was never a shortage of UN staff from various agencies to volunteer to undertake the two- to three-hour drive to Bureh Town. The drive was an adventure in itself; we would pass through tiny villages where houses were made of mud and wattle. Women could be seen gathered around the village well, conversing as they fetched water. Or they would be sitting around communal fires, cooking for their families. The sights provided us with a peek into the day-to-day lives of the locals.

The tropical climate contributed to lush vegetation that covered the track down to the cove where the beach was located. Our lively group would bring an array of delectable treats for the beach, including chicken to barbecue, salads, cakes, beer, water – and fresh oysters, foraged from the nearby rocks.

Our R&R cycle was every six weeks; at that interval, we would take a week out to decompress and gather our energy to tackle the monumental work that was required to put Sierra Leone back together. Like other missions, when a group of people are thrown together in a highly volatile situation, we seek those with similar experiences, which frequently results in lifelong friendships being forged. One such friend was Livio, an Italian who was employed by a sister agency and had worked all over West Africa. He had invested in a home in South Africa as his go-to place. His wife and child lived there, so returning home for him took just a half-day of travel.

On one of the trips that Beh and I took to Pretoria, South Africa, Livio invited us to visit him and his family in Uvongo. He had raved about his place for a long time, and he wanted us to see the splendor of his home and its surroundings for ourselves. He hadn't exaggerated – it was a stunning spot, and we were immediately taken by its charm, its proximity to the Indian Ocean, and the perfect climate there.

When we returned to Freetown, we began planning our next R&R back to Uvongo to explore the possibility of purchasing a home there ourselves. We reserved a room in a cozy hotel in the charming beach town of Margate, setting the stage for a long weekend. Livio was a gracious host and an amazing chef; he cooked us some of the most wonderful dinners while we were sitting around the deck. We also tasted a selection of the best wines of South Africa. Livio told us some amazing stories, including a fascinating anecdote about preparing dinner for Pope John Paul II himself. Of course, not to be outdone, I was able to regale him with my story of meeting the pope in the UN General Assembly Hall in New York.

As our visit progressed, we decided to check out the local real estate market, albeit without any concrete intentions. We had a set of criteria in mind – a view of the ocean and a pool to bask in during the sun-kissed South African days. Livio recommended a real estate agent, who guided us through a selection of homes, each more stunning than the last. We were really impressed when we entered a house that seemed to embody all our wishes – it was perched overlooking the Indian Ocean, boasting a stunning landscaped garden and an infinity pool that blended seamlessly into the horizon. We viewed several other stunning homes, and it was not an easy decision; but we both agreed that this particular house was outstanding. We put in an offer, which was immediately accepted. Within a few weeks, we were the owners of the stunning house overlooking the Indian Ocean – our own piece of Uvongo's beauty and charm.

House in Uvongo, South Africa

Beh and I had been together for 13 years by that time, and I was never more happy in my personal life. I had the love and companionship of a wonderful man, something that had evaded me for many years, and something I had wished for my whole life. There was never a doubt that we would spend our lives together. There were no demands and no niggling annoyances. We found that we almost knew each other's thoughts, and we could each sense when something was going wrong – instinctively providing personal space, if necessary.

We were blissfully happy during our time at home in Uvongo, and we went there to celebrate my birthday in 2005. I thought Beh was acting suspiciously when he left the house several times, coming back a few hours later each time. On the day of my birthday, he cooked dinner; we sat on the veranda and popped open a bottle of champagne. When we toasted my birthday, he produced a beautiful diamond ring, placed it on my left ring finger, and asked me to marry him.

Later, after our return to the United States, we were married in Milford, Pennsylvania, by a justice of the peace. It was May 29, 2007, with just the two of us and two witnesses. It was as perfect as anything I had ever wished for – a confirmation of our commitment to each other and our deep love. We scheduled the wedding celebration for July, when we invited family and close friends to join us in the Hotel Fauchere, around the corner from where we had made our wedding vows.

But back in 2003, we had been almost three years in Sierra Leone when Beh's hunch was confirmed – he received word that his work had come to an end on the mission, and we found ourselves once again packing bags and arranging to transport our possessions. Sierra Leone was reasonably stable by that time, with the peace accord holding, and the negotiations with the rebel groups resulted in the decommissioning of arms.

Democratic Republic of the Congo

After a short trip back to New York for meetings at headquarters, our next mission would take us to the Democratic Republic of the Congo (DRC), a vast country whose size is almost 25 percent of the United States. The Congo was once ruled by King Leopold II of Belgium, who established the Congo Free State by brutally commandeering the land. It was not enough that Leopold controlled the Congo as a colony, similar to other European powers. No, Leopold privately owned the region – it was his personal fiefdom. Publicly, the king's goal was to bring civilization to the people of the Congo – but the reality was very different. The population was forced to work to extract valuable resources, including rubber and ivory, for Leopold's personal enrichment.

Estimates vary, but at least half of the Congolese population died from maltreatment, which included amputations and malnutrition. In 1908, public criticism and international pressure forced the king to turn the Congo Free State over to the country of Belgium. The newly-named Belgian Congo remained a colony until it gained independence in 1960,[1] and then became known as Zaire. Then, in 1997, after President Kabila ousted the authoritarian regime of Mobuto Sese Seko, he changed the country's name to the Democratic Republic of the Congo (DRC).

The DRC has never really known peace; and since the 1990s, armed groups have been part of the political landscape of the eastern part of the country. Communities created militias to defend themselves in response to foreign-backed armed groups, which were accused of using war to loot the country's natural resources. Tensions between Rwanda and the DRC date back to the genocide of 1994, when the minority Hutu tribe slayed more than 800,000 Tutsis in a six-week murder spree. Thousands of Hutu perpetrators mingled with Tutsi refugees fleeing to the DRC for safety. Once elected, the post-genocide Rwandan government launched military operations in a bid to force the perpetrators back home to face justice, believing that the DRC was providing refuge for those behind the massacre.[2]

The DRC is a rich country with mining resources that include copper, cobalt, gold, diamonds, coltan, zinc, tin and tungsten. Those resources allow for the manufacture of consumer products such as textiles, plastics, footwear and cigarettes. And the minerals for materials needed for the ever-growing demand for electric cars – cobalt, lithium, manganese, nickel and graphite – mostly come from the DRC, although little of the vast wealth trickles down to the Congolese. Most of the population lives in dire poverty.

King Leopold had introduced the French language to the Congo, and it became the official language for education and government (alongside the four national languages). In 1999, the UN set up a mission known as MONUC – an acronym for the mission's French title. The role of MONUC was to address the ongoing conflict and insecurity in the region, to promote peace and stability, to protect civilians affected by the conflict, and to support the disarmament, demobilization, and reintegration of armed groups – while facilitating the delivery of humanitarian assistance.

MONUC's UN headquarters was based in the DRC's capital, Kinshasa. My task was to establish the Board of Inquiry to investigate and report on death, serious injury, and traffic accidents that involved UN staff, military, and civilians in the mission.

Chatting with a colleague one day, she commented on my career trajectory, implying that my life must have been charmed to land me in such a prestigious position. Of course, she knew nothing of my start in life as that little girl from Krasne in the hand-me-down clothes, who, despite the myriad challenges, had the will and ambition to continue and keep pushing. Indeed, I had come across many fortunate people working in the UN; but not all employees had climbed out of poverty and hardship – many of my colleagues were the children of diplomats and professionals. The conversation with my colleague made me realize that I was the exception, and I needed to recognize just what I had achieved. I cannot deny that there also had been a certain amount of luck and a lot of hard work involved to get me where I wanted to go.

Thinking about my history, I realized that I was still carrying the lost child – holding onto memories and emotions that no longer served me. The hurt and the hardship of my childhood had defined my thinking, sticking to me like velcro. I needed to let go of the negative emotions that had influenced my decisions and limited my growth. It was necessary to embrace the woman I had become and acknowledge that I had outgrown the struggling teenager, the beatings and punishments in the home of my adoptive parents, and the loneliness of my childhood as an immigrant in a foreign land. I was now a completely different person – with peace of mind, confidence, and happiness. I could hold myself in the company of kings and queens, prime ministers, and plain ordinary folk. That realization allowed me to let go of the grip of the past; and as I did so, a weight lifted slowly from my shoulders.

In the DRC, Beh was deeply involved in his role. He was meeting with department heads, government officials, and warlords, negotiating a way forward to bring peace to conflict-ridden regions of the Congo. His fluent French allowed him to converse without the need of a translator, and in turn, he gained the confidence and trust of those he was negotiating with.

As violent outbreaks randomly and frequently raged in the area, our home was nestled within a safe and secure community – an oasis in that troubled country. However, not only was staying physically safe often a challenge, the DRC was also an incubator for all sorts of tropical diseases: malaria, dysentery, cholera, and dengue. And there was always the possibility of spider or snake bites. Sometimes, despite taking every precaution, there were staff members that came down with some of the diseases. So, it was necessary to keep a careful watch on personal hygiene and call upon the mission doctor right away if there was any sign of illness.

We were tucked away in a small house with a charming garden, where all types of tropical flowers constantly bloomed. The garden brought a sense of the resilience and continuity of nature, despite everything that was happening around us. I found solace in this patch of land as I watched nature, uninterrupted, in our peaceful refuge. It was a simple dwelling, but the cozy atmosphere it provided made it a place we could call home.

The long hours we both spent in the office provided us with the luxury of a house cook, Albert. While Beh had no issues communicating with Albert, I was a different matter altogether. There was frequent hilarity as I tried to communicate with this lovely man in my schoolgirl French. We would both end up having a fit of the giggles, as I tried to use sign language along with my basic language skills. Not only did Albert possess a good sense of humor, he was also an excellent chef. So, arriving home from work in the evenings was pure joy – dinner would be cooked and ready to eat.

Beh's work would frequently keep him occupied into the late hours of the night, and I often found myself alone in the evenings. The sound of drums could be heard in the distance as a blanket of darkness descended over the city each evening. The rhythmic beats became a nightly serenade for me, a reassuring reminder that we were indeed in Africa, and privileged to experience some of the rich local culture in the DRC. For all their troubles, the Congolese people have a rich culture that includes music with popular genres that spread across Africa, and also became popular in Paris, France. *Soukous* is the most famous genre; it grew out of 1950s Cuban rhumba rhythms with jazz. *Kwassa kwassa* dance rhythms are found in the clubs and bars of Kinshasa.

There was seldom a weekend that Beh was not occupied with duties in the office, and that allowed me to meet up with friends to explore some of the vibrant and creative scenes in Kinshasa. The city was teeming with art galleries showcasing modern African art – expressive work from creative geniuses. The art resonated with me; it compelled me to become lost in the world of colors, shapes and stories. In addition to the art I viewed in the galleries, I encountered Congolese locals selling African trinkets on the bustling streets. Captivated by the fine details and cultural significance of these objects, I could not resist purchasing several pieces. To this day, these pieces continue to bring me joy in my own home, reminding me of the work and creativity that brought them to life, and where I purchased each one.

Exploring Kinshasa one weekend, I stumbled on the Thieves Market, in the heart of the city. It was a large open area with row upon row of old wooden tables displaying a treasure trove of unique and fascinating artifacts. As the only white person, and therefore, the only blonde in the bustling market, I stood out among the vibrant colors in the lively market atmosphere. When I stepped into the maze of aisles, an array of statues and trinkets unfolded before my eyes. From intricately carved wooden masks to brilliantly painted pottery, each item seemed to tell a different story, each a representation of the rich cultural heritage of the DRC.

In order to navigate the bustling maze of goods and vendors, I was fortunate to have the companionship and guidance of a local and trusted friend who knew the ins and outs of the stalls, and kept an eye out for any untoward attention. I was well aware of my privilege in the situation, having the knowledge and security provided by my local friend. The stall holders, skilled in the art of negotiation, presented their wares with pride and invited me to explore the treasures. It was a brief but fascinating glimpse into the lives of some of the people in the local tribes, which provided me with a greater understanding of some of the hardships that had crippled the resilient and beautiful country. It was an event that left a lasting impression; each artifact and trinket represented a link to the Congolese people and their spirit.

The art objects that I brought home were not merely souvenirs, but a spark of my memory of the Congo that will stay with me forever. The Thieves Market would not have made the UN security list as the safest place in Kinshasa, so I was not advertising my excursions there at work. I was aware, though, that on my own I would be an easy target for any pickpocket or criminal.

Even so, I was always on the lookout for a taste of adventure. Turning a blind eye to the rules of our UN security officer, I was delighted when a colleague suggested we try a spa day in Brazzaville, in the Republic of the Congo, the neighboring country to the west. Brazzaville is directly across from Kinshasa, separated by a body of water. The idea of crossing the mighty Congo River for a day of R&R to unwind in the neighboring country sounded like a worthwhile escapade. So, we were all enthusiastic about dipping our toes in Brazzaville for the day.

We rose early to see the morning sun rising, painting the sky with hues of gold as we reached the port. A local man was preparing to transport goods across the river, and we negotiated a decent rate to persuade him to take us across. We were like excited schoolchildren as we boarded the barge. The Congo River is 4,370 kilometers or 2,720 miles long, just shorter than the Nile, and the third largest river in the world. It is the only major river to cross the Equator, and a hugely significant part of life for both the DRC and the Republic of the Congo – transporting goods, providing livelihoods for fishermen, and creating opportunities for women to gather socially on its banks to wash clothes for their families.

Brazzaville is a smaller city than Kinshasa, with a population of just over one million. The city welcomed us with a blend of new sights, sounds, and smells; and its atmosphere offered a refreshing contrast from the intensity of Kinshasa. My friend and I ventured to a local spa, where we spent the morning being pampered with manicures and pedicures. The fatigue from our hectic work schedules was washed away and the experience left us rejuvenated. We then took off to explore the city; we strolled through the streets, absorbing the vibrant energy and diverse culture. Stopping off for lunch in a charming café, we tasted some of the delicious local delicacies before taking a taxi back to the river's edge. The barge owner was waiting for us, ready to take us back to Kinshasa.

Our two years in the Congo passed in a blur of work and exploration. We made the most of our R&R cycles, where we took the opportunity to return home to Uvongo, and as always it allowed us to decompress and reenergize. During our time in Kinshasa, we made the most of every moment, embracing the challenges and rewards that came with the mission; but like all things in life, our time there came to an end. As we prepared to leave, I reflected on our time in the DRC. Our perspective had expanded there and had gifted us with unforgettable memories.

Unfortunately, conflict continues in the DRC to this day, and the population continues to receive few benefits from the huge mineral resources. The country's valuable resources are used in the manufacture of electric cars, smartphones, and other electronic goods that make our lives easier. Today, the valuable resources there are mostly controlled by the Chinese, who stepped in when the government sold off the country's wealth to the highest bidder. However, there was no trickle-down effect to most of the Congolese, and most of them still live in abject poverty.

While the goods from the DRC provide us with greater access to more electronic assets, the catastrophic effects caused by the mining industry across the country has resulted in the death of an estimated six million people since 1996[2]. The Chinese mine owners promote child labor, impose horrific working and living conditions, and are involved in systematic evictions of residents who live on the vast mining concessions. The air and water around the mines are contaminated with toxic dust and waste from mining processing, and millions of trees have been cut down due to the industrial activity.[3]

---

2 https://www.aljazeera.com/news/2024/2/21/a-guide-to-the-decades-long-conflict-in-dr-congo#:~:text=Approximately%20six%20million%20people%20have,internally%20displaced%20in%20eastern%20DRC.

South Africa

E ven though we were leaving the Democratic Republic of the Congo (DRC) with some regret, a new assignment was waiting for me in South Africa. I was to serve as field operations officer, overseeing a team of local personnel in Pretoria. The unit's mission was to facilitate medical evacuation cases from the DRC. We were to act as a link between the government of South Africa and the UN in the Congo operations to ensure that staff members who became ill received the best possible treatment. They were taken to some excellent facilities in South Africa.

This assignment brought us closer to our home in the Kwazulu-Natal region. We were delighted with the prospect of spending more time in our little paradise, even though it was a 700-kilometer distance between headquarters and Uvongo. We flew between the two places at every available opportunity. It was such a privilege to be able to invite family to visit and enjoy some of the beauty and delights of Uvongo. A highlight of our time there was a safari in Kruger National Park, where we explored the wilderness and witnessed majestic creatures in their natural habitat. It was four unforgettable days, sleeping in basic huts and hotels inside the park, where we were roused from sleep with the sounds of animals welcoming a new dawn.

When my mission was coming to an end and we were preparing to leave, I contacted UNFPA to explore potential job opportunities upon my return. In my absence from New York, there had been a new department created, the Office of the Security Coordinator – and as luck would have it, there was a position available. My experiences and responsibilities in the field gave me a good advantage for getting the position; and after a series of online interviews, I was offered the job.

Time quickly passed and we took to the skies again, arriving back home to the streets and sounds of New York. Even as the plane touched down, I felt a sense of homecoming, ready to welcome the next opportunity. Our journey had come full circle; Beh and I settled into our life in Manhattan, resuming our routines. As we walked the familiar streets, we once again found ourselves absorbing the energy of the city that never sleeps. Central Park became our oasis, offering a change from the hustle and bustle. Broadway shows delighted us with their entrancing performances, and our friends from the United Nations filled our weekends with laughter and companionship.

New York offered a feeling of belonging, but I knew that our adventures were far from over. The experiences we had gathered from around the world had enriched us beyond measure, creating a tapestry of memories that would forever hold a special place in our hearts.

Epilogue
Florida

The longer that the rift between me and Dana continued, the more difficult it became to reconcile. My sister Joanna always kept me informed of what was happening in Dana's life; she informed me of the birth of Dana's two boys, Dane and Tyler – which made me a grandmother. It broke my heart not to have the opportunity to bond with the two boys as babies. My enforced absence prevented me from having the opportunity to spoil my only grandchildren when they were small.

Dana was stubborn, and her hurt went as deep as my own. Joanna, who acted as a go-between, often expressed sadness about our estrangement and would regularly speak to Dana about a reconciliation with me.

Eventually Dana sent word that she would reconcile, and so I called her. She explained that she called me not because she wanted a reconciliation, but because she wanted her children to have grandparents, and she felt her boys were missing out.

She was still living in Chicago at the time, and I flew to meet my wonderful grandchildren, who were ages 6 and 4. I received only a polite reception when I arrived at the house, but the joy of meeting and connecting with my two grandsons would not allow my happiness to be diminished.

Over the intervening years, the relationship with Dana repaired; but it never quite recovered to the degree of the days we had spent in Maputo or on our trip to Poland. I think Dana has never fully forgiven me for wanting a career. I feel that she was looking for, and wanted, a traditional mother who stayed home and was present when she arrived back from school.

I was obviulsly not attuned to Dana's growing resentments and her reaction caught me off guard. But I felt that she would listen to and respect her father. I believed she felt she had been abandoned, and I knew her father would provide the stability and discipline she needed. After our meeting in Chicago, I needed to explain my motivation and what had driven me to shoot for the stars in terms of my career. My experiences of poverty as a child in Krasne – when the family was unable to pay for a simple funeral for my mother – ultimately led to my decision that financial independence was the only thing that could provide me with freedom.

I wrote to Dana and apologized for my decisions, explaining that they were made in her interest to provide for her material needs. I added that, in no small way, decisions were also made because of my fear of poverty. Dana believed she suffered because of my decisions, but in the end, she had the benefit and love of her father with stability in the home. Probably, because of my own traumatic childhood, it was something I just could not provide.

I completed over 31 years of service with the United Nations in 2010, and together Beh and I came to a decision that it was time for retirement. I could have continued for several more years, but life is too precious to be dictated solely by work. Besides, we wanted to travel just for pleasure without the possibility of receiving an email or a phone call to attend to some emergency.

We began retirement by taking an extended weekend trip to Florida to visit family and friends. The trip opened our eyes to the possibility of a new chapter in a warmer climate, closer to our relatives. My sister Joanna lives in St. Petersburg and my other sister Teresa lives in Cape Coral. Also, Beh's daughter and her family live close by in Boca Raton.

When we left home for the trip, we were knee-deep in snow and blistering cold winds. In Florida, we savored the sunshine and visited a delightful community there, enjoying the company of friends. Feeling the warmth on our bones, we began considering the prospect of escaping the freezing winters and the sweltering summers of New York.

It was also time to say goodbye to our home in Uvongo in South Africa; it had served us well for a decade as a refuge from some heart-wrenching, stressful work situations. We took one last trip there to gather our belongings and ship them back to the US; the furniture and artifacts were all reminders of our life as nomads across continents and conflict zones.

We decided that Florida was where we wanted to spend our sunset years, so we trolled the 'net to see what houses were for sale and then set up real estate appointments. We set about viewing about a dozen houses, but one stood out that had captured our interest – a charming house where the sunlight danced through the windows. The house spoke to us and we both instantly fell in love with it. We recognized the potential to put our own stamp on the home, with just a few adjustments.

Our Florida home became a place of peace and contentment, where Beh
would often lounge by the pool or beach. I would be occupied lunching
with friends, immersing myself in new hobbies and activities, and taking
theater classes. We also had the luxury of the opportunity to travel, visiting
family and friends in Europe and beyond. We were enjoying the fruits of

our work, appreciating our good health, and feeling gratitude to have come through so many wars and conflict zones unscathed.

As January 2020 unfolded and the COVID-19 virus made its ugly appearance, we, like so many others, were gripped with fear. On the news, we watched Asia and Europe drowning in the virus, contending with rising death tolls, and running out of burial places. We realized it was only a matter of time until the virus arrived on our own shores.

On the evening of March 13, 2020, we had a dinner party with friends, and as we bid them farewell that evening, we were unaware that it would be our last evening together for several years to come. After working so long with the United Nations, we had grown to respect the wisdom and science of our colleagues in the World Health Organization, and so we heeded their warnings. We supported each other by securing vaccination appointments, recognizing that precaution was our lifeline for survival. While some friends succumbed to the disease, we managed to make it through – a little battered, but surviving the storm once again.

The virus was still prevalent when, in May 2021, I was dealt a blow – the results of a mammogram indicated that additional tests were required. Then, a phone call from my doctor confirmed the worst when he mentioned the word "cancer." It left me reeling in fear and panic. I found out that I had cancer in both breasts, and just to be unique, there were two different types of cancer, adding layers of complexity to my treatment. I was not going to wait around – I made an appointment with the oncologist the following week.

A week after going through a lumpectomy, surgery was booked to remove lymph nodes under both arms. That procedure was followed by radiology to ensure that the cancer cells were completely removed from my body. I was lucky to have the gift of family and friends for support during that time, as well as the constant support and love of my beloved husband – who was at the start of his own journey with health issues at the time.

* * *

As I was finishing this book with the publisher, my beloved husband passed away. His presence will forever be etched in my heart, a gentle reminder of the love we shared and the moments we cherished together.

In loving memory of my beloved husband

Behrooz Sadry
(1936 - 2024)

Book Club Questions

- What was your favorite part of the book?
- Did the book inspire you to take on challenges that seem insurmountable?
- Did the book spark your interest in finding out more about the countries in which the author worked?
- Which scene stuck with you the most?
- What did you like/dislike about the writing?
- Did you reread any passages?
- Would you want to read another book by this author?

About the Author

Christine Sadry was born in Poland during the oppressive communist era and immigrated alone to the United States at just 9 years old. As a first-generation immigrant, she faced numerous challenges, but persevered to build a new life. Christine forged a career as an international civil servant, dedicating 30 years to her work at the United Nations, where she contributed significantly to global initiatives. Her story is one of remarkable resilience and determination, reflecting the strength and spirit needed to overcome adversity and succeed against the odds.

www.ingramcontent.com/pod-product-compliance
Lightning Source LLC
Chambersburg PA
CBHW022218020425
24281CB00004B/21